The Power of Karma

The Power of

Karma

HOW TO UNDERSTAND YOUR PAST
AND SHAPE YOUR FUTURE

Mary T. Browne

WILLIAM MORROW
An Imprint of HarperCollins*Publishers*

HarperCollins books may be purchased for educational, business, or sales promotional use. For information please write: Special Markets Department, HarperCollins Publishers Inc., 10 East 53rd Street, New York, NY 10022.

FIRST EDITION

Designed by Kelly S. Too

Printed on acid-free paper

Library of Congress Cataloging-in-Publication Data
Browne, Mary T.
    The power of karma : how to understand your past and shape your future / Mary T. Browne.— 1st ed.
      p.   cm.
    ISBN 0-06-621293-6 (alk. paper)
    1. Karma. I. Title.

  BF1045.K37 B76   2002
  291.2'2—dc21   2001045245

02   03   04   05   06   RRD   10 9 8 7 6 5 4 3 2 1

For Lawrence

CONTENTS

ACKNOWLEDGMENTS

With gratitude and respect to my editor, Jennifer Brehl; my agent, Jan Miller, and her staff, with a special thank-you to Michael Broussard; and to my sister, Sheila Browne.

The Power of Karma

What Is Karma—and How Does It Affect Me?

Karma is the universal law of cause and effect. You reap what you sow. You get what you earn. You are what you eat. If you give love, you get love. Revenge returns itself upon the avenger. What goes around comes around.

Literally, "karma" means "action." Good action equals good karma. Bad action equals bad karma. Each individual is solely responsible for his or her own actions, and every action will produce a reaction equal in every way to the suitability of the action.

Karma is justice. It does not reward or punish. It shows no favoritism because we have to earn all that we receive. Karma doesn't predestine anyone or anything. We create our own causes, and karma adjusts the effects with perfect balance.

Many people think there's nothing they can do to change their karma—it's preordained so why bother trying to change their situation? This is what scares people. These folks think that to accept the reality of karma one must be passive. It simply isn't true. Karma is active. We can—in the blink of an eye—make decisions that will shape our futures and transform the parts of our lives that are causing us unhappiness.

Think about karma as a bank. The Karma Bank is an impartial, honorable, incorruptible, infallible solid establishment. Every single person in the whole universe has an account in this colossal depository. Each time you perform a positive action, you add good karma to your account. Every negative action that you perform produces bad karma. The ultimate goal is to have your account in perfect balance. When this is achieved, you will have mastered your karma.

Introduction

I have used my psychic gift to counsel people for over twenty years. In that time thousands of individuals have come to me for private sessions. Most of my work involves helping people identify their problems and, once those problems are acknowledged, suggesting solutions. I do not control anybody's fate. I've spent a great deal of time reviewing the most prevalent issues on the minds of my clients, friends, and acquaintances. Whether the person is a CEO of a Fortune 500 company, an Oscar-winning actor, a lawyer, a psychiatrist, a Wall Street broker, a telephone operator, a secretary, a student, a mother, or a journalist, a common thread runs through everyone's life. Individual circumstances vary, but the needs are similar: Everybody longs for health, love, security, and balance. However, the paradox is that too frequently people believe that these goals can be most effectively achieved through manipulating sex, money, and power. People come to me hoping that my psychic gifts can help them by predicting the best way to achieve their desires.

The main focus and passion of my work has always been, and remains, my one-on-one private consultations with people from all walks of life. Over the years my practice grew so large that it became impossible to see everyone who requested a private reading or healing. Something had to be done. Writing was the most practical way to share my knowledge and experience with a wider audience.

My first book, *Love in Action,* was inspired by a session with a client who told me, "I came to you today because I am trying to find God." People came to me for many reasons. A few came merely out of curiosity. Some had specific questions, such as, "Will I marry my current boyfriend?" "Which job offer should I accept?" or "How many children do you see in my future?" But this was the first time someone asked me to help him find God.

It was the end of the eighties—the "me" generation. People were feeling empty, a deep spiritual void. In that book I shared my belief that the most direct route to God was through serving others in any way one could. A person did not have be Mahatma Ghandi or Mother Teresa in order to live a useful life. One did not have to be a do-gooder or a doormat in order to live a life of service. Every action performed to help another is a step closer to God—each individual life is of equal importance. *Love in Action* presented the reader with a spiritual approach to freedom and happiness.

Life After Death was written because one out of two clients asked me to help them understand what happens when we die. Not since a war had history seen the tragic death of so many young men and women. In my opinion, depression leading to despair, illnesses like Parkinson's disease—which previously had been reserved for the elderly—and the AIDS epidemic were some of the most common reasons for people's surging interest in the afterlife. Having the ability to psychically see visions of the afterlife gave me the firsthand experience to write this book. The continuing positive response to *Life After Death* proves to me that people *can* overcome the fear of the death, resulting in a greater appreciation for the sacredness of life.

And now I'm writing *The Power of Karma* because at this time the most frequently asked questions by my clients, and at my lectures, concern the law of karma and how it has a direct impact on their daily lives:

1. Is everything in our lives predestined?
2. I do everything that I can to be a good person, so why is my life such a mess?
3. Will I ever find my soul mate?
4. Why did my mother die of cancer? She was the kindest person who ever lived.
5. I do all my boss's work, yet he's never grateful and earns twenty times what I do. Why is this happening to me?
6. I starve myself, go the gym, count every calorie, and I'm still thirty pounds overweight. My doctor says my thyroid's fine. Why is my body like this?
7. He swore he loved me. Why has he never called again?
8. Is it cheating if you have sex with someone on the Internet?
9. I went to an astrologer who told me I was born to be famous. When?

10. Do you believe in reincarnation? I had a past-life regression and was told that this was my last life on earth.

11. I want to leave my husband for my boyfriend. Will this come back to haunt me?

12. Why me? Am I paying for something I did in a past life?

Magazines, newspapers, TV, and the movies are using the word "karma" as often as they once used the phrase "what goes around comes around" or "you get what you deserve." A word that many people believe fits only into an Eastern or New Age vocabulary has become an absolute part of our vernacular.

It became crystal clear to me that an explanation of karma, reincarnation, predestination, and free will was desperately needed. The fantasy that things happen to us by chance, by the luck of the draw, that we live only one life, that some omnipotent force makes choices for us, and that we have no power to make decisions for ourselves had to be dispelled.

There is a distinct call for a practical way to understand how karma works and how we can work our karma. There can be no karma without reincarnation, so the inextricable link between these two doctrines has to be thoroughly explained. Karma and reincarnation have remained enigmas for too long. No lasting transformations—physical, spiritual, or psychological—are possible without the knowledge of karma and its direct impact on all aspects of our lives. Visualizations, affirmations, positive thinking, healing meditations, invocations, or any other such practices are a waste of time unless we understand karma first.

An understanding of balance is paramount to our study of karma. To live in balance means to have inner peace and at the same time to be at peace with your external world. It is harmony. In one way or another, people lack this—some have perfect health but no money, some have fabulous sex but no job, some have money but bad health, some have power but no love.

My personal philosophy that everything is karma is the leitmotif of my life. Through sharing my passionate belief in karma and reincarnation, I believe that people will begin to learn patience with themselves and others. After all, what's the hurry? We have eternity in front of us. There is plenty of time to learn to grow and find happiness. We can just do the best we can with whatever situation is presented to us.

Even as we face difficult times and know we will probably face more arduous ones in the future, the opportunity for spiritual growth is enormous. We must remember that everything is karma, and the shape of our future is in our hands.

1. Karma

The depth of people's confusion about karma doesn't surprise me. Ask ten people the meaning of the word and you'll get ten different answers. "Doesn't it mean destiny?" "Wasn't that a word used in the 1960s at Woodstock?" "I think karma means I did something wrong." "Isn't it something to do with the Buddhists?" "Oh, yeah, it means fate!" Most people know that the Ten Commandments come from the Bible, but they have no idea where karma originated.

Karma and reincarnation are the principal doctrines of Buddhism and were also taught by systems of esoteric philosophy such as the Pythagorean and Platonic schools. But for our practical purposes I will begin with Adam and Eve.

ADAM AND EVE

The need for health, sex, money, and power was born the moment the spirit entered the physical body and was forced to live in the material world. The defining moment occurred when Adam and Eve were banished from the Garden of Eden.

They were given everything with one condition: Do not eat the fruit from the Tree of Knowledge of Good and Evil. They ate the fruit. They broke the law. They paid the price. No god *dictated* their karma; they brought it upon themselves. Adam and Eve were banished from their perfect life. From that moment on, everybody had to work hard to earn happiness. There was no more free lunch. Materiality then became a necessity for spiritual accomplishment. Simply put, we had to work for our food and shelter, deal with personal relationships, face health problems, and die.

Karma was born when mankind was born. The story of Adam and Eve is a metaphor for the spirit being incarnated into a physical body. "Eden" could be another word for the spirit world—a place of beauty and harmony where the soul exists after the body dies. Adam and Eve's banishment gave us our schoolroom for the soul's development. The physical world gives each one of us myriad opportunities to learn ultimately how to live in balance—harmony. The karmic strokes that seem harsh often turn out to be the best things that could happen.

YOU MAY BE WONDERING HOW I KNOW ABOUT KARMA

First, as a psychic, I have an innate belief in the law of karma. My psychic gift gives me the ability to perceive things without being told. Karma always made perfect sense to me. Second, my studies of Buddhism, Hinduism, Judaism, Christianity, and Theosophy support that belief. Third, in-depth discussions with my Master Teacher confirm that karma is the only practical, sound, sensible, comprehensive, intelligent, logical, down-to-earth, matter-of-fact, sane answer to why good things happen to bad people or why bad things happen to good people. Fourth, I have seen the effect of karma in action in my life and in the lives of every person I've encountered.

Whether people understand the law of karma or not, everybody is subject to its effects. For example, you didn't see the No Parking sign, but your car was ticketed anyway. You tried as hard as you could to convince the cop it wasn't your fault. However, you still got the ticket because you broke the law. Ignorance of the law was no excuse. Who among us has not experienced something like that?

MY CURIOUS KARMA

Some people are born to be singers, doctors, scientists, or painters, and others are born with psychic gifts. Hundreds of people have asked me, "Why were you born psychic and not me?" I can give no answer except "I was born with a psychic gift. I must have developed it during past lives. It's my karma to choose how I handle it in this one."

This gift, like all gifts, is useless if the recipient does nothing with it. An acorn will never grow into a tree if it isn't planted. It has taken motivation, discipline, introspection, patience, tenacity, and humor to shape my gift into a vehicle to help others. People with psychic gifts have existed since the beginning of humankind.

The first truly psychic experience I remember occurred when I was seven years old. My sister and I had moved to Iowa to live with our Grandma Grace. My Great-aunt Mayme owned the town's funeral parlor. One day she asked me to come over to answer the phone for her. After telling me exactly what to do in case a call came in, she left. Taking my job quite seriously, I sat in her office and stared at the phone. Not much time passed before restlessness overcame me, so I took a walk around the funeral parlor. Without knowing what had brought me there, I found myself drawn to one of the rooms, in which a wake was scheduled for later that day.

It was early, so no member of the deceased person's family had yet arrived. Still feeling too timid to enter, I stood outside the room in which the casket lay, perceiving a silence that had the quality of quiet one feels upon entering a church. Flowers and the waxy smell of candles filled the room. Suddenly a floral arrangement appeared to float in the air. For a moment the flowers seemed suspended in space, and then, ever so gently, they began to move through the room. I closed my eyes, then opened them again, expecting the apparition—which must surely have been a figment of my imagination—to have disappeared. Not so. The flowers were still suspended in air. Then I saw the ever-so-faint shadow of a woman holding the bouquet. She smiled radiantly, waved with one hand, replaced the flowers in their original spot, and disappeared. At that point I walked straight up to the coffin. The person lying in the casket was the woman who had been holding the flowers. I was not afraid. I felt great excitement flowing through me. In that moment I was filled with certainty that there was no death. When I told my grandmother what had happened, she merely nodded as if she understood. She told me not to mention it to anyone, because most people would not believe me. "You have a gift. Be grateful for it," she said. Grandma Grace was a very practical woman. She had a deep belief in her Catholic faith. She had never talked about any psychic phenomena. My curious gift was not fostered in my home environment. Yet Grandma's simple confirmation that it was okay to be psychic was enough for me to feel secure about it. I never felt the need to ask her specific questions about psychic abilities. I also knew that Grandma had said all that she was going to say on the subject.

One of my closest childhood friends reminded me that my ability to locate missing objects with great accuracy began when we were children. Someone would say, "I can't find my keys," and I would reply, "They're behind the third book on the shelf in your bedroom." Off she would go to see if the keys were there. Inevitably the person would return with the keys and say, "How did you know?" There was no rational explanation how I knew, because I'd been nowhere near the person's house. You may think it odd that I accepted my ability so easily. I was taught not to boast, and it was normal for me to find things. It was just part of me. This happened so often that those who were close to me became used to it and took my ability for granted. Nobody made a big deal out of my psychic gifts. I think this is a major reason I've always been very comfortable with myself. Upon finding a journal of mine that was written when I was twelve, I was surprised to read, "I know that I have lived before and that I will live again." It seems I believed in reincarnation before even hearing the word. Although Grandma confirmed that I had "a gift," she never referred to past lives, and there were no metaphysical books available in our Iowa town. There is no environmental or scientific basis for my belief in the ancient philosophy of reincarnation. It just made sense to me that I'd lived before.

I was a creative child, singing at a very early age and always very interested in theater. After graduation from high school I went to the University of Iowa to study music and drama. At school I had a part-time job working at a bookstore. It was there that I was first exposed to books on metaphysical subjects, especially works concerning karma, reincarnation, and life after death. The interest remained with me after I left college and moved to New York.

My first years in New York were divided between pursuing the theater and studying metaphysics. My psychic abilities were becoming stronger and sharper, and I developed an overwhelming desire to help people. Sitting through auditions, I could always tell who would get the part merely by looking around: I could see in my "mind's eye" who would be chosen. I'd look at a person and just know. Often we had to wait a few hours to be seen by the director, and I spent my time giving psychic readings to people I met there. It would just happen; I'd start talking to someone, and psychic information would come through. Others in the room would overhear me talking, and before long a crowd would gather. Actors are known to be very open-minded, so they were quite accepting of my gift and grateful for the readings.

At this point in my life I desperately wanted some guidance but didn't know where to find it. I did not need anyone to teach me to be *more* psychic. I needed help in learning how to handle my abilities and how to use them in the best possible way. Studying on my own, I became passionate about the teachings of Helena Petrovna Blavatsky. From a Russian noble family, in 1873 she came to the United States, where she founded the Theosophical Society. Endowed with extraordinary psychic gifts, she traveled and studied in Tibet and wrote extensively.

Her most famous work is *The Secret Doctrine*, which explains, in-depth, karma, reincarnation, science, philosophy, and religion. The recurring message is this: The greatest reason for living is to be of service to humanity. Karma allows us to master ourselves and learn to live in balance with all of nature. Reincarnation and karma are the only sensible explanations for the seemingly illogical events with which our lives are fraught. If you accept this teaching, then it follows that you believe there is no such thing as a victim. We only attract situations that we ourselves have created. There is no such thing as "luck"—good or bad—because nothing happens by mere chance.

I'd reached the stage where I could not serve two masters: theater and my desire to help people by using my psychic gifts. At this time I closed the door on my theatrical pursuits, and from that moment on, word of mouth brought clients. It was a big change for me, but one I've never regretted.

There is an old saying that goes "When the student is ready, the teacher appears." I worked with clients for a little over a year before I was introduced to my Teacher. I call him Lawrence, though that's not his real name. I do this in order to honor his right to privacy, but I have altered nothing about his teachings.

MY KARMA WITH LAWRENCE

My first awareness of Lawrence, my Teacher, came through a recurring dream. I was about ten when it began. The dream went like this:

I was in a house, sitting calmly on a mat on the floor. I was uncertain about the exact place, but it appeared tropical because there were lovely palm trees and exotic flowers arranged in pots. I was calm and quite at home in this simple house. A very tall man with the deepest blue eyes I'd ever seen walked into the room and held his hand out to me. I took his hand and studied his face, somehow knowing that I must remember his exact features. Then, as if he'd been able to read my mind, he smiled and said, "I am your Teacher. You will not forget me. We will meet in person when the time is right."

My first in-person encounter with Lawrence was over seventeen years ago, on a glorious spring day in New York's Central Park. I was compelled to go to the park by the psychic "inner voice" that is part of my gift. This ability to receive messages by hearing someone speak clearly in your head is called clairaudience. I awoke with the message "Get dressed and go to Central Park as quickly as you can." I arrived with no definite expectation.

I sat on a bench, unaware of Lawrence's presence until he addressed me by name. I turned toward his voice, and a shock of recognition went through my whole being. This was the Teacher I'd dreamed about since early childhood. I was both reverent and thrilled. He took my hand and immediately calmed me.

Lawrence is a man, a real person, not a ghost. He is very tall, quite thin, and he appears to be in his early fifties. He never seems to age. He has the most beautiful blue eyes I've ever seen, with a depth of understanding and compassion that seems unearthly. Yet it isn't his outward appearance that sets him apart from other men; it's his inherent spirituality, his aura of total harmony. I must stress that it is Lawrence's decision whom he meets and when a meeting is necessary. Many people have asked if I could introduce them to my Teacher. I can answer only that it is not in my power to do so. Lawrence has complete control of his emotions and can at will perform amazing psychic feats. He never displays these talents without a very good reason. He emphasizes that the use of psychic powers can be dangerous and unsettling unless the motivation is to teach or to serve. Throughout the years since my initial meeting with Lawrence, we have met in many places around the world. In a way I feel like a soldier who receives orders and proceeds to follow them without question, knowing that the reason will be revealed at the right time. Yet most often his communications aren't in person. Sometimes he contacts me through letters or phone calls. But most of the time Lawrence communicates metaphysically, by sending powerful thoughts to me. When he does this, I hear his voice and he gives me help or instructions as I sit quietly and listen to his messages.

I call him "Master," even though he once said to me, "My child, to those who have found their true spiritual self, there is neither master nor student. Such a person regards every person with equality. You must find the master within yourself and share this discovery with others. This is a part of your karma. In this way they, too, will be blessed with a life of inner peace and balance."

PARIS

One of our meetings took place in Paris. I received a letter from him instructing me to go there. He told me to meet him at a specific time at the entrance to the Rodin Museum. We walked the museum together, examining the masterpieces. "The greatest art is that of living," he said.

We studied the shapes of the sculptures. Lawrence spoke

knowledgeably about the works of art and the history of the artists. His knowledge of art is that of a scholar, and it is coupled with a reverence for the artist's talent and beauty of the work.

"It takes many lives to develop a talent such as Rodin's," he said. Lawrence compared these sculptural masterpieces by Auguste Rodin and Camille Claudel to our own lives. These works of art took the shape of a hand, a screaming child, a couple making love, a man immersed in deep thought. They'd all begun as marble, stone, or clay. The artist's thoughts had transformed these materials into magnificent shapes, inspiring profound and varied emotions in the observer.

"All life is a work of art in progress. Everyone has a great deal of power to shape his own future. A great sculptor would not aimlessly cut a stone. He would decide the form he wished to produce and then proceed to mold his work of art. A wise person is one who thinks before he acts or reacts," Lawrence said.

We talked about karma and reincarnation and how our past lives affect our present. Three times he stressed that we learn the most about our past lives by examining our present one. Lawrence said, "These artists make their own creations and mankind makes its own destiny."

Lawrence left Paris a few days ahead of me. He told me to return to the Rodin and to spend time contemplating the sculptures. He promised that we'd see each other very soon. "You will understand why I chose this particular meeting place." I returned to the Rodin Museum and slowly studied each work of art. I stood in front of *Le Penseur* (*The*

Thinker) almost in a state of meditation. And then it came to me. The complete realization that we have the power to shape our futures and control our karma on levels we never imagined hit me like a thunderbolt. The idea to share my experiences—past, present, and future—started to take form.

Lawrence, in his profound yet pragmatic way, is an enormous help in guiding all of us by imparting his extraordinary wisdom. I once asked him about personal responsibility versus individual karma. He smiled and answered, "My child, if you see a drowning man, do you refuse to save him, thinking it's his karma to die? Or jump in and rescue him because it's your karma to help him to live?"

I answered, "I'd rescue him because it's my karma to be in a position to do so. Maybe it was the person's karma to feel fear, or to ruin his clothes—*not* to die. Karma is a two-way street. It's the responsibility of each one of us to do whatever we can to help anyone who is in placed in our path."

Lawrence added, "You would have created very bad karma if you allowed someone to drown while you had the ability to save him."

MY SIXTH SENSE

There is a great deal of confusion concerning psychic abilities. For some people the word "psychic" carries weird connotations: images of Gypsy fortune-tellers looking into crystal balls, ouija boards spelling out messages, tarot card readings, and tables levitating at séances bringing greetings from the departed are but a few.

Ever since Noël Coward's brilliant play *Blithe Spirit*, the public has related to his model of a spiritual medium in the character of Madame Arcati. Margaret Rutherford played his ideal medium as an eccentric, zany, rather dotty, bicycle-riding channel for transmitting spirit messages. One of my goals is to dispel such misconceptions. I'd like to take the mystery out of the metaphysical but leave the miraculous intact. One of the most common misconceptions is that a psychic and a medium are one and the same. Nothing could be further from the truth.

A medium is a person who is the conduit or channel of transmission between the living and the spirits of the dead. A psychic is able to receive information that lies outside the sphere of the five senses. This is why psychic ability is also known as the "sixth sense."

Any messages I receive from the departed come into my head, in my mind's eye.

Here's the way my psychic gifts work. I look at a person and perceive facts in his or her life without being told. For example, a person sits down and I'm able to "know" his occupation, personal relationships, fears, state of health, or place of birth. This information sometimes comes to me in pictures. This is known as *clairvoyance*.

Most often, words come into my mind, a form of the psychic gift called *claircognizance*. Claircognizance is a mental sense of awareness in which information spontaneously flows into the mind without the aid of sight or sound. Another form of the psychic gift in which information comes to me is *clairaudience*. Simply put, this means "clear hearing." It is the faculty to hear a vocal message in one's head, not audible to those without this psychic sense.

Besides predicting future events, I can also discern how the past is affecting present or future circumstances. During a session I predict the likeliest probability based on a client's present behavior. Free will can always intervene and cause another outcome, thus changing the karma. For example, I see an actress getting a part in a Broadway play if she goes to the audition. She doesn't go to the audition. Her decision results in no part. She changed the karma by her own action.

It's very important in my work to be aware of how much a person can take at one time. Everybody has a different capacity and temperament. Certain people who are very ill want to know every detail I see about their health situation, while others don't want to hear everything at once. My responsibility is to tune in to the person and speak in a way that is comfortable and productive. Firmness and honesty must be tempered with empathy and kindness. There are times when being tough is being kind. Many people are frightened when they come to see me; they think that I will be the bearer of tidings of impending doom.

Common sense tells us that if we see something wrong on the horizon, we can take necessary steps to avoid it. Things that appear disagreeable at the time of a reading are not always, in retrospect, bad news. Let's say I see a woman in a relationship with a dishonest man. I tell her details that prove I can define his character. She doesn't want to hear that her beloved is a bad egg because she's hoping they will marry. I tell her to take time to find out more about his behavior. She may be disappointed by the news, but time proves that the reading was accurate. She ends the relationship. It hurt at the time but saved her a great deal of grief in the long run.

If I see that a client has a medical problem, I advise him to see a doctor immediately. A psychic reading does not take the place of a physical exam. Psychics are not doctors, and responsible ones never try to give medical or psychological advice that is the province of medical professionals. You can tell a client if you see a physical or mental problem, but he must follow that up with the proper medical consultation. Some people have an illness and have seen twenty doctors with no success in finding the root of the problem. I can give them my "read" on their situation, and they can check it out with their physician.

Lyle and a Grain of Salt

Lyle looked dreadful when he came to see me. He'd been ill for over a year, and no doctor had found out what was wrong with him. He was at a point of despair, unable to work and feeling as if he were losing his mind. I sat looking at him, and the word "salt" came to my mind. "This may sound crazy to you, Lyle, but I think you have a salt problem," I told him.

"What do you mean?" he asked, looking at me with disbelief.

"I can't tell you anything more, because I don't see anything else. Please ask your doctors to check your body for a salt problem."

Lyle called two months after our session. He'd gone to the Mayo Clinic for a complete checkup. He asked them to see if there was any problem linked to salt. On the last day the doctors found that he had a salt imbalance. He is now feeling terrific, back at work, and very grateful.

There are times during sessions with clients when I do receive messages from their departed loved ones. I never try to pull spirits toward the physical world, but if it's the karma of a person to receive a message, she will be given one. There is no trancelike state; I am always totally aware of what I'm saying to the person in front of me. When I receive these messages, there are no spirits in the room with me. My insights come from the sacred gifts of clairvoyance and clairaudience. I see pictures or words in my mind's eye. Often I'm able to focus on an "astral screen," using a form of psychic concentration that allows me to break through the barrier between earth and spirit. I am aided in this process by my spirit guide, White Feather.

WHITE FEATHER

White Feather has been introduced to my readers in my first two books. Many people have asked me questions about him. They confuse my relationship with him with my relationship with Lawrence. These two are as different as night and day.

White Feather is a spirit guide. He isn't a teacher, but a

protector and a connector. He protects me from negative influences when possible and helps with the connection between earth and spirit.

This large Native American friend came into my consciousness frequently during my childhood. I was in my twenties when I first learned his name. He impressed his name upon my mind clairaudiently. In my head I heard a strong, clear, precise voice: "I am White Feather. If you need me, invoke my name. I will never be far from you. I have followed you since your birth." White Feather is from the Dakota Sioux tribe. I think a good adjective for him would be "no-nonsense."

He doesn't stay with me all the time. He just gets things done and then goes on with his other business in the spirit world. All psychics and mediums have spirit protection. It's a great honor to be given the name of your guide. So, yes, he's a ghost or a spirit; call him either. You have to be psychic to see him, because he does not have a physical body, just a spirit one.

We are living in a world where people are desperate to have spirit guides. Sometimes the first question a client asks me is "Do you see my guides around me?" Most people who ask about guides are lonely, bereaved, or misinformed. They are clinging to their friends or relatives who have "passed over" into the spirit world. That's why people think their grandma, uncle, husband, wife, lover, or godparent may be acting as a spirit guide. People seek advice from the dead because they aren't confident with their own judgment or with the living. A wise person will acknowledge that communication between worlds is possible but will wait until karma decides to give him a message. Very few people have a spirit guide. Yet we all have the ability to reach toward our higher selves for guidance. This ability develops out of learning to listen to the voice within that comes from going into the silence. You can ask your higher self to give you the strength to learn from all your experiences. To do this requires no assistance from the spirit world. White Feather makes no decisions for me. It's my karma to have his help with my psychic work. I have great reverence for this great spirit. I never take his assistance lightly, or expect him to do things for me that I must do for myself. Let me reiterate: It's a karmic inheritance to be given a spirit guide, not the result of a mere desire. People who have spirit guides have earned them.

After psychically perceiving an individual's issues, I suggest practical and spiritual methods for resolving them. There are many problems we can avoid by understanding that all our actions and reactions are shaping our lives. If we act in harmony with life, the good karma of love, health, fulfillment, security, happiness, and inspiration will be ours. But in contrast, the bad karma of unhappiness, illness, insecurity, and discord is attracted into our lives when we act with disharmony.

It has been said that a picture is worth a thousand words. So let me give you a picture of what it's like to have a private consultation with me.

Beth Saves Her Sinking Ship

Beth arrived, and I immediately perceived that she was headed for a divorce. She and her husband had stopped communicating on all levels, and both felt deep resentment toward the other. There was a real power play going on between them. "Beth, if this behavior continues, it will result in a divorce," I predicted. She sat quietly and then said, "Lord, things are bad between us, but I don't want a divorce." I was able to make her aware of her negativity and "saw" that a last-ditch effort could save this relationship. Beth said she'd give it her best shot. "Please," she pleaded, "give me some suggestions, because I don't know how to go about changing this situation."

I replied, "First, you have to make a firm decision that you will change your nasty behavior into positive action. Second, stop blaming your husband for everything. You are both part of the problem. Third, be kind, listen to him, count to ten when you feel like yelling. Fourth, buy yourself a journal and make a list of all the good things in your marriage. Put your three children on the top of the list, and go on from there. Writing things down and contemplating them makes them more real."

"I never told you that we had three children, or that I get really nasty with my husband and find myself yelling at him." Beth seemed taken aback as she said this.

"That's my job, Beth. I'm supposed to know things that I haven't been told," I answered. This knowledge helped her trust my guidance. She asked me to go over my suggestions again. Handing her some paper, I told her to write them down. Beth left with her notes and a firm decision to save her sinking ship.

Ten months later Beth returned to see me. I was impressed by her positive attitude. "Mary," she said, "our last session together had a healing effect on me, and I swear, it rubbed off on my husband." They both started to treat each other with respect and kindness. It wasn't easy, but they changed their karma and saved the marriage.

PRACTICAL TOOLS

To get the most from *The Power of Karma,* you would be wise to purchase a few things. It's not essential, but I guarantee you will have greater success in shaping all areas of your life if you do so.

1. A *Power of Karma* Journal

Buy yourself a journal. This journal/notebook can be lined or unlined, colored or white. It's not necessary to spend a lot of money on your book, just purchase one that you really like. Label it *The Power of Karma,* and use it in conjunction with this book.

Don't panic and don't fear—you won't be asked to write more than you are able to do with ease. I have found in life that if we are asked to do too much, we end up doing nothing. My own experience has taught me that writing things down can be an invaluable source of help. It would have been impossible for me to re-create incidents in my life if I hadn't kept journals. I couldn't have seen my own personal struggles and victories if I hadn't kept a record of my life. So get the journal. You will discover how effective it is.

2. Colored Index Cards

You will need **colored index cards**. These cards will be used in conjunction with chapters two through six. I suggest you use these colors:

Karma and Reincarnation	**White**
Health	**Blue**
Sex	**Pink**
Money	**Green**
Power	**Purple**
Balance	**Yellow**

We'll be using these cards throughout *The Power of Karma* to jot down reminders, affirmations, prayers, and practical suggestions. Think of them as spiritual bookmarks. They will help us as we change negative behavior to positive, thus creating new good karma. All text to be written on index cards will appear in boldface.

For example, take out a *blue* index card and write down this powerful affirmation:

Uncontrolled anger creates negative karma. It is destructive to my health, my work, my friends, my family, and my soul. I will find ways to control my rage.

You will place these index cards somewhere easily accessible and read them as often as you can. As I said, they make excellent bookmarks, fit nicely in a pocket, and can be placed with a magnet on the refrigerator door or framed on your desk. Just keep them close and go over them until you integrate the words into your very soul. The only other physical tool you'll need is your favorite writing instrument.

Throughout the book I will be suggesting various spiritual exercises:

1. Meditation

Most people have tried to meditate but give up because they are too busy. You needn't take hours out of your day for meditation. In fact, a few minutes can be more effective than trying to set an exact period of time to do this. Meditation is an activity of thought, a positive state of mind. You don't have to blank your mind or close your eyes in order to meditate.

Concentrate on an idea or an image. Almost anything can become a subject of meditation: love, strength, forgiveness, security, or balance. The only essential condition for meditation is that you must not let another care or problem interfere with your thought process. You must hold the thought steady in your mind. This can be done while you are engaged in other activities, such as waiting in line at the store or bank. You can hold on to a thought, but you must never lose sight of your surroundings. Meditate on love or harmony while you're waiting, and the time will pass with greater ease. You can meditate before going to sleep by allowing the mind to flow toward thoughts of forgiveness or compassion. This will help you to sleep with greater peace and in time awaken with this serene state intact.

Through meditation we can use our power of concentration to cast out bad karma or to construct good karma in our lives. We have to accept that in our days of rushing and turmoil, time has become a valuable commodity. However, once we understand the power of meditation, we will find moments to practice this habit. Any activity performed with complete concentration, upon the completion of that one activity, is a form of meditation. Cleaning out a drawer can become a type of meditation. You must do this task with calm dedication, until the activity is completed. Your thought remains on the drawer, not on the mailman or the need to go to the store, answer letters, or make dinner plans. Every time your mind flows away from the process of doing the action in front of you, you bring your thought back to the drawer. We will explore many meditations throughout the text.

2. Examination

This is a mental exercise that asks us to look at ourselves. It demands courage because it's painful. All that is required is that we spend some time looking, in an intense manner, at some specific part of our life. The object of our examination can be anything: emotional responses, the use of our time, behavior toward others, and so on.

This exercise helps us to understand parts of our lives that have been difficult to assimilate. My Teacher, Lawrence, is a learned man, and has often quoted Plato: "There can be no greater tragedy than living an unexamined life."

What is an unexamined life? It is living with no idea of

why we are doing what we are doing or why we have done what we've done in the past. It's never stopping to think before we act. A person living an unexamined life will say, for example, "I don't know why . . .

I'm depressed.
I can't find true love.
I drink too much.
I can't find a career that makes me happy.
I never finish anything that I start.
I feel tired all the time.
I'm not treated with respect.

Try this simple examination: Every night before going to sleep, examine the events of the day. This is a type of spiritual checkup. If you determine you've acted out of balance, creating bad karma, vow to do better tomorrow. This exercise will become clearer as we practice different forms of examination throughout the book.

3. Visualization

This is the method of using your imagination to create a picture in your mind. You must put yourself into a relaxed, focused state of reflection. For example, picture yourself happy. Do not put a specific person, event, material possession, or any desire into the frame. Just see yourself walking down the street, sitting by the ocean, lying under a tree, or looking at the sky. Don't restrict your happiness by making it dependent upon anything or anyone outside yourself. Hold this picture; enjoy the calm, tranquil, balanced feelings that are flowing. Repeat a few times a day. This is one simple example of a positive use of this technique. I will share many other ways to use your visualization ability to change your karma from bad to good.

4. Affirmation

An affirmation is a statement of spiritual truth intended to help us overcome a false attitude. This is a technique based on the repetition of a single positive sentence or phrase (for example, "Day by day, in every way, I am getting better and better." Emile Coué).

5. Prayer

Most people use prayer as a means of asking for something they have not earned: "Oh, God, please make him call me." "Please let me win the race." "Please let me hit the lottery." "Please make my car start." True prayer is an acknowledgment of the higher self that is in each one of us. The prayers used in this book will be ones that support our desire to be more compassionate, sympathetic, understanding, secure, and balanced people.

6. The Number Forty

Throughout the book the number forty will play a big part in the time needed to try a plan for reshaping parts of our life. It could be forty seconds, minutes, hours, days, weeks, or months, in order to implement a specific change. Every number or amount used in this book is specified for a reason, whether it be under direction from Lawrence, from repeated personal experience, or from historical evidence.

For example, I use the number forty because it has a strong metaphysical force behind it. It is a number of completion. Moses spent forty days on the mountain, and Jesus was tempted for forty days in the desert. It rained for forty days after Noah built the ark, and the Israelites spent forty years wandering in the desert. Lent lasts for forty days, and Jesus remained dead for forty hours before he came back to life. Life begins at forty. There are forty pillars at Stonehenge arranged in a circle that has a diameter of forty steps.

2. Karma and Reincarnation

Karma has been given a bum rap for a long time. I believe the basis of this injustice lies in the fact that most people can't really make heads or tails of it. Karma has been deeply misunderstood. It's common to blame it when people feel they've been dealt a bad hand. "It's my karma, so I can't help being angry/lonely/broke/depressed/misunderstood/professionally unfulfilled." Human nature tells us to point a finger at anyone or anything *except* ourselves for the shape our lives are in.

Don't you think it's odd that people rarely credit karma for the good things in life? It's highly out of the ordinary to hear anyone say, "I've got great karma. I have a terrific family, good health, lots of friends, enough money, and a great job. I must be doing something right."

Remember as stated earlier, the doctrine of karma teaches

that everything that happens in nature is dominated by the law of cause and effect. You reap what you sow. You get what you earn. You are what you eat. If you give love, you get love. Revenge returns itself upon the avenger. Literally, "karma" means "action." Good action equals good karma. Bad action equals bad karma. Each individual is solely responsible for his or her own actions, and every action will produce a reaction equal in every way to the appropriateness of the action. For example, if you put your hand into the fire, it will be burned. The fire isn't to blame. Your lack of good judgment caused the pain. Once, we hope, is enough to learn the lesson: Be careful how you handle fire.

Take out two *white* index cards and write:

1. Karma means action. Good action brings forth good karma.
2. Karma means action. Bad action brings forth bad karma.

Don't forget that karma can be good as well as bad. Fire can be used to keep us warm or to cook food that can be shared with others. People see more retribution than reward because their own behavior has been more selfish than selfless. We don't have to wait for good karma. We can make it now. Every moment is an opportunity to shape our lives into ones with greater karmic balance.

Take out a *white* index card and write:

I see more bad karma than good when my behavior is more selfish than selfless.

Karma isn't something outside of us. We are our karma. Heavy stuff? You bet. But it will change your life once you understand the beauty and fairness inherent in this Divine Law.

Take out a *white* index card and write:

I am my karma.

Karma is justice. It does not reward or punish. We will suffer for pain that we have caused, and we will reap joy from the good we've produced. Karma shows no favoritism in life, because we have to earn all that we receive. We are what we are because of our past actions, thoughts, and desires. We are building our future through our present behavior. Karma doesn't predestine anyone or anything. We create our own causes, and karma adjusts the effects with perfect harmony.

Take out two *white* index cards and write:

1. I am what I am because of my past thoughts, actions, and desires.
2. I am building my future by my present thoughts, actions, and desires.

There is not a sorrow or pain, joy or delight that can't be traced to our actions in this or a former life. Noble actions and constructive thinking create positive karma. We produce good karma anytime we are optimistic, compassionate, thoughtful, and kind. This results in a life with greater love, security, and balance. If you sow good seeds, you will reap a good harvest.

Take out a *white* index card and write:

Noble actions and constructive thinking create positive karma.

Love attracts love, generosity brings forth abundance, and the force of positive action results in the good karma of happiness and balance. In contrast, if we think or act in an irresponsible, selfish, greedy, thoughtless, revengeful, mean-spirited, or unkind manner, we are creating bad karma. The consequences of such negativity are discord, insecurity, and turmoil. Our actions do not have to be evil in order to cause us or others to suffer pain as a result of our behavior. Many times a minor lack of consideration results in hurting others.

KARMA: THE UNIVERSAL BANK

I'd like to repeat what I said about karma earlier: The Karma Bank is an impartial, honorable, incorruptible, infallible, solid establishment. Every single person in the whole universe has an account in this colossal depository. Every time you perform a positive action, you add to your account; each negative action produces a deficit. The ultimate goal is to have your account in perfect balance. This means that your account is only positive: no deficits and no bills to pay.

Each individual is completely responsible for his or her own investments. There are no excuses, like "I forgot to make a deposit, so my check bounced." Remember, this is an impartial bank, and ignorance of your mistake won't protect you from the result of the action. You will pay the fee for the overdraft, no matter what the underlying reason might be. Nobody will care that you didn't remember to balance your account or that you just didn't know how to do it. You'll learn one way or another that you, and only you, are responsible for your karmic bank account. You'll get what you earn.

We must never use past-life karma as an excuse for our lack of judgment in our present life. Take, for example, someone who ignores his income taxes for years—gets away with it. Then one day a letter arrives from the IRS billing him for the back taxes, plus interest. It might have taken years, but sooner or later the debt came due. You can plead poverty, beg for mercy, blame the mailman for not delivering or the dog for eating your tax returns, but you *will* pay the piper. Perhaps your wages will be garnisheed or your property confiscated, or you may even go to jail, but they will collect what they are owed. You can plead "unfair" until pigs fly, but you will be forced to pay. Because it's your karmic debt, and yours alone.

We have to face the fact that, for better or worse, for richer or poorer, in sickness or in health, until our physical death and into our next life, everything, past, present, and future is karma. We create good or bad karma by our thoughts and actions. This isn't an obscure, abstract, New Age spin. It's practical common sense. Your karmic bank account is a synthesis of what you are doing at this moment as well as what you have done in the past. The future is there for us to shape in any way we choose. We can confront our problems and strive to find solutions, or we can go on and on repeating the same dumb things over and over. The Karma

Bank will not forgive your debts. Nor will it charge you for things you aren't responsible for. There are many people who have had serious trouble with their credit rating and found the strength and discipline to get themselves back on track. Similarly, we can learn ways to keep our karmic accounts in good order, to lay the groundwork for future prosperity, spiritual as well as financial.

You are your karma, so you own your own Karma Bank. Forget about blaming anyone or anything for your liabilities. They are *your* problems to solve.

It's of utmost importance to remember karma goes both ways: Take the credit for your wise decisions. The good things that come from having a secure account are *your* perks; nobody else will receive the credit. The Karma Bank can't be corrupted. You reap what you sow and get what you earn. What goes around comes around. All that is yours will come to you.

YOU CAN'T TAKE IT WITH YOU—OR CAN YOU?

We all leave our karma account on earth when we "pass over" into the spirit world. You don't create karma while you reside in the spirit realms. The balance in your account, be it plus or minus, is exactly as you left it the moment the physical body died. Your spirit will be reborn, and you will have your account in place, as you go forward and choose to add or subtract from it. This explains the apparent injustices of life. Any sensitive person has to wonder why one man is born into wealth and power and another who appears far more deserving has had to struggle through poverty and humility. Or why one person is born blind and another with twenty-twenty vision. It's all in the karmic bank statements!

THE AKASHA

We have heard of a memory bank, a place where the subconscious stores data not immediately accessed at will. Your personal karmic bank account has its complete records stored in the Akasha. Imagine an enormous library with records of all transactions ever made by anyone in any lifetime. The Akasha is an invisible region surrounding our universe. In this region a record of everything that has ever happened in the cosmos is stored. It can be thought of as a "psychic library" that holds an infinite amount of data. Every thought, action, and reaction that each of us has experienced in any of our lives is stored in the Akasha.

AVOIDING THE KARMIC BOOMERANG

There is something called a karmic boomerang that is a very important element of this book. The boomerang is an action that backfires on its instigator. In other words, you get hurt in the same way you intend to hurt someone. Not all boomerang effects are immediate. Some take weeks, or even years, to manifest.

Many people think they can do what ever they feel like doing, no matter how selfish, and they will get away with it. Nothing could be further from the truth. For example, a curse returns upon the one who utters it, or upon his innocent relatives or friends who breathe the same atmosphere with him at the time the curse is uttered.

Stella Has a Big Bang Boomerang

A client of mine, Stella, cursed a person of whom she was very envious. She banged her fist on a table and yelled, "I hate her! She has everything and I have nothing. I wish that she were dead!"

"Control yourself, Stella. Don't ever talk like that," I said. "Don't you understand how dangerous it is to spew this type of rage and negativity? It's evil. It could backfire and cause harm to you or those close to you."

"I don't care. I hate her!" Stella arrogantly replied. There was nothing I could do, because her reason was destroyed by her irrational anger and jealousy. Months later I learned that Stella had lost her job and depleted her savings, that her husband had left her and her mother had had a serious stroke. The woman she had cursed was doing just fine. It broke my heart to learn that Stella had brought all this upon herself.

Stella's "big bang" boomerang gives us a frightening look at how quickly certain karmic actions can backfire and result in personal disasters. But don't fool yourself, we are also accountable for the matter-of-fact things in daily life—things we barely think about. Have you ever snapped at a coworker or friend who didn't deserve it? This negativity doesn't just disappear. It will boomerang back upon you in some way. You will pay for your lack of respect by having someone else disrespect you.

Lois Is Forced to Face the Music

Over a decade ago, twenty-eight-year-old Lois seduced Morris, a wealthy, married man with two children. He divorced his wife of twenty years and married her. Last year Morris left Lois for a woman young enough to be his daughter. Boomerang. It may have taken over ten years, but Lois ended up in the same boat as Morris's first wife. She was stunned, but she had to face the music. She vowed never again to allow herself to become involved with a married man. And Morris has a terrible relationship with his children because of his selfish behavior and to this day is a very unhappy man. Boomerang.

Here are a few surefire tips to help you to avoid the painful boomerang. Write them down in your *Power of Karma* Journal and memorize them.

1. Think before you act.
2. Treat people the way you want to be treated.
3. Don't take things that don't belong to you (for example, spouses, jobs, bank accounts).
4. Your soul records every action. You can't get away with anything.
5. You get what you earn, so work for love, security, and balance.

6. Revenge returns itself upon the avenger. Never seek vengeance.

KARMA IS LINKED TO REINCARNATION

The law of karma cannot be separated from the doctrine of reincarnation. Reincarnation, which is also the basis of my teaching, tells us that we live not one life but many. We return to the earth until we have achieved, through our own labor, "perfection." Perfection is a state of total selflessness. All desire for physical pleasures is replaced by a complete dedication to serve humanity. Man is, in essence, a composite of all his lives but must learn to focus on how best to live the present one.

Karma and reincarnation are completely interwoven. Each one of us is making karma, good or bad, in every thought and action we produce. Reincarnation, and our lives in the physical realm of earth, gives us the schoolroom to balance our karma and, ultimately, to master ourselves.

Through a series of lives we are given the opportunity to shape ourselves into beautiful, peaceful, fulfilled, loving, selfless people. Experiences not remembered are not lost. They are part of our minds and exist in feelings, attractions, tastes, and dispositions.

Life is a continuation, not a termination. We "pass over" from the physical world to the spirit world with all the experience we have gained throughout a succession of lives. We rest in the spirit realms until our soul is ready to gather more knowledge. At that time we are reborn into a physical body in order to proceed with our education and to further balance our personal karma. We claim our karma bank account and continue working toward balancing it.

I'M NOT COMING BACK

Many people who are currently experiencing difficult lives may find the idea of coming back to earth distasteful. I've heard numerous people declare, "I'm not coming back." What they're really saying is, "I'm not happy."

They are in pursuit of happiness and feel hopeless to achieve their goal. I've tried to help my clients understand that one life is no more adequate to gain the experience necessary to promote happiness than one day of school would be sufficient to earn a college degree.

The fact remains that we will be reborn into the physical life until we have completed our education and become perfected persons. We will return to earth to reap the results of all our actions and to gain further knowledge and wisdom as we journey toward self-mastery. We are born to achieve this state of complete balance: mental, physical, and spiritual. When that is earned, it will no longer be necessary to incarnate on the earthly plane.

Let me clearly define self-mastery:

- perfect physical and mental health
- control of all forms of psychic phenomena

- the ability to understand all languages
- total courage in every situation, even when life threatening
- complete selflessness
- absolute faith in the law of karma

I have learned from the Akasha, from studying the ancient wisdom, and from discussions with Lawrence that the process of mastering ourselves takes approximately eight hundred earth incarnations. The only person whom I know that has reached this state of development is Lawrence.

INTERVALS BETWEEN REBIRTHS

The length of time between incarnations varies. A baby born into a land of famine, living a few hours or days, may be reborn almost immediately. This little soul will have had no time to create any good or bad karma in this present, short life.

A great soul who is needed to help humanity in a precise way may be reborn more swiftly than usual. This great person would agree to an early return to earth because of his or her passion to serve mankind. Examples of this type of service would be the need to head a certain religion, to create a vaccine that can save millions of lives, to bring forth a musical style that would have a healing effect on the nervous system, or to serve the needs of a nation's political karma. These great services to humankind would demand a person of tremendous spiritual character or extraordinary experience and talent. The higher the level of spiritual development a person earns, the more control he or she has over the time and place of rebirth.

A philosopher such as Pythagoras, great teachers such as Gandhi or Blavatsky, or a musician of Mozart's genius may not reincarnate for thousands of years. This is because it may take that long to find a suitable environment to support such a person's accomplishments. These great people serve mankind by inspiring us from the spirit world. They are always contributing in some way, be it on the physical earth or from the spirit world.

Many people have misconceptions about the time it takes for most of us to reincarnate. Clients have asked me, "How will I know where to find my child/mate/relative/friend if he or she is reborn before I die?" Let me stress that most of us normal people (as opposed to true geniuses or great teachers) stay in the spirit world from eight hundred to twelve hundred years. It is unlikely that your loved ones will return to earth before you pass over. Our loved ones will be waiting for us when it's our turn to make the transition from the physical world to the spiritual realms. As we walk through the valley of the shadow of death, we will have no fear, because we will see the people we loved on earth who passed over before us waiting to help us make the transition.

HOW ONE READS THE AKASHIC RECORDS

As I explained earlier, all information regarding our past lives is stored in the Akasha. An enormous amount of my knowledge concerning karma and reincarnation has come from my psychic ability to "read" the Akashic records. This aspect of my psychic gift allows me direct access to information about people's pasts, in this life and other ones. It also can be a way to find out how people who are in the spirit world are doing.

In order to access accurate information about one's past lives, it is necessary to read the Akashic records. This takes a special type of psychic concentration and a great deal of energy and practice. There have been times when I was able to penetrate the walls of this so-called library and read specific records regarding an individual with relative ease. And there are other times it is difficult or impossible for me to break through the barrier into this cosmic memory bank.

The reason for this inconsistent ability to pull up Akashic records is twofold. First, it's simply a matter of not always having the psychic energy that is needed. Second, there are things we're not supposed to know, so the information will be obscured.

But the Akashic records are often helpful. For example, one of my clients has an exceptional child. This boy started reading at the age of three—without being taught. When he was four, he played very complex piano pieces, also without the benefit of instructions. Neither parent plays any musical instrument, and, in fact, the father is tone-deaf. I was able to help them understand him by looking into his Akashic records. I saw that this little soul had been a prodigy in his last life. Luckily for the child, his parents do believe in reincarnation. Their belief that the child brought these talents with him from a past life makes it easy for them to nurture his abilities in the here and now.

Not all past-life issues are as obvious as this child's talents. I've seen people with phobias, such as fear of water or the dark, that appear to have no basis in this life. These usually are brought in from a past life. The karma remains that we must fight to resolve these issues in our present life. It's a waste of time to get angry because you can't remember past lives. Who can remember what they were thinking when they were three months old, let alone before you were born?

Take out two *white* index cards and write:

1. I will not waste time getting angry because I can't remember my past lives.
2. We learn the most about past lives by looking at this one.

Another client, Jim, had an obsession with big-band swing music that led him to believe that he'd lived in the 1940s. He was born in 1955, so he would have had to be reborn almost immediately if his feelings were true. During a session I was able to determine information about his departed grandfather. Grandpa played Benny Goodman and Glenn Miller music all through Jim's mother's pregnancy. He continued playing this music until he died, when Jim was two years old. Jim had no recollection of this but found out that it was true when he asked his mother. It turned out that Jim wasn't experiencing past-life karma but present-life acquired taste.

The law of karma teaches that whatever happens to us, for good or ill, is just. We attract only what we have earned through our personal choices in this and all our past lives. It has taken us many lifetimes to accumulate the karma we are experiencing in this present life. It's just common sense that there is simply not enough time to work through all of our karma in one lifetime. We can only try to do our best with whatever circumstances are presented to us now. The past has happened; you cannot change that. You can change your attitude and behavior today and in the future. People who don't have the knowledge of reincarnation may not understand the meaning of certain events in their lives. They may believe that life is unfair.

CAN WE PROVE REINCARNATION?

The number-one reason people don't believe in reincarnation is their inability to remember their past lives. The majority of people, like Jim, can't even remember the first few years of *this* life. Most minds are not yet sufficiently developed to remember back beyond a certain point. Try to remember what you were feeling during the first six months of life. After doing this little experiment, it may appear more obvious why most of us can't remember our past lives.

Many people believe that their souls are immortal. There is no scientific proof of this, but it is accepted. I'm sitting at my computer writing and breathing. I can't see the air, but I'm certain it's here. We accept many things without demanding evidence.

Abilities can be greater confirmations of past lives than memories. The child musical prodigy Mozart, the genius Einstein, the marvel of the three-year-old reading and writing without any tutoring, are wonderful examples of past-life talents brought into present lives. I've had American clients more at home in Italy, France, or Egypt. They just feel at home somewhere else, and in fact they probably lived there in a previous incarnation. There is a definite reason we are born into a certain nation, but it's possible that we had happier, longer, richer, past lives in other places. This would explain the seeming paradox of being incarnated into one country while feeling a greater affinity for another ethnic group.

"Everything was very familiar. I'd walk down streets and recognize houses I'd never seen before. I spoke fluent Egyptian within three months of my arrival. You would have sworn that I had studied the language for years, even though it was the first time I'd ever studied Egyptian. It was unsettling, but it made me believe in the possibility of reincarnation," one American client living in Egypt told me.

Take out a *white* index card and write:

Abilities can be a greater confirmation of past lives than memories.

Jessica Conquers Her Fear of Water

Jessica came to me trying to discover why she's terrified of water. There was no incident in this life that could explain her phobia. She'd tried everything in her search to overcome her irrational fear—swimming lessons, therapy, and hypnosis, to name a few. Nothing helped her. Her parents were positive that nothing had occurred when she was too young to remember.

I told Jessica that her fears were very likely the result of an incident in a past life and that I'd try to see if I could get any past-life information for her. I made it very clear that I can't always get this type of information. I focused my gaze on a corner of the room and felt a familiar intense pressure across my forehead and through my eyes.

I was able to break through into the Akashic records and see that Jessica had drowned in a large sailing boat. I knew it was Greek because I saw a name painted on its side *The Seiren*. (It turned out this is Greek for "mermaid.")

I watched a series of pictures in my mind's eye and saw a great storm come up with no warning. Everyone on the ship was lost. The pictures faded. I looked at Jessica and told her that was the only information I could give her. She related that she'd always been terrified of going to Greece. She added, "I always felt that if I went to Greece, I'd die there."

I told her not to worry—that the drowning had already occurred. She still held a subconscious memory of this traumatic incident. The past-life information I was able to receive brought the incident to the surface. Time would tell if this would help Jessica overcome her phobia.

I'm happy to report that Jessica did conquer her fear of water. One morning shortly after our session, she awoke and the fear was gone. Jessica couldn't explain what had happened. She said it was as if the phobia had never been there. Her parents were shocked when Jessica told them she was going to the beach with her boyfriend. She took it slowly but was able to wade into the shallow part of the ocean the first day at the beach. In time she learned to swim, and she's even planning a trip to Greece with her family.

The truth of the past-life reading was shown through the reaction it had on Jessica's phobia. She was able to let go of her fear because it was based on an incident that had already occurred. Jessica received that message because she had earned the karma to be helped with overcoming her fear. Remember, just because something is a problem at this moment doesn't mean it has to remain so for your whole life.

Take out a *white* index card and write:

A problem that I have right now does not have to remain one my whole life.

DÉJÀ VU

Déjà vu is a French term that literally means "already seen." This feeling of déjà vu occurs when a person senses that something she's doing for the first time has happened before. Such feelings often occur on the first visit to a strange place. A place may be so familiar that one recognizes streets and houses she's never seen before in this life. Other situations may involve people we've never met. There is an immediate rapport, or revulsion, or a sublime familiarity that makes us feel we have been with this person before.

Lawrence told me, "All true déjà vu experiences are linked to something from a past life that is unresolved. You should take time to identify and explore your déjà vu experiences."

Take out a *white* index card and write:

A true déjà vu is linked to something from a past life that I must resolve.

Connie's Déjà Vu

I've had many clients over the years talk about their feelings of déjà vu. A lady named Connie comes to mind. She came to see me shortly after returning from a trip to Maine. Connie was walking on the beach and met a man named Ken. She looked at him and was overwhelmed with a feeling of relief. "I wanted to cry out to him and ask him where he'd been. I was overcome with emotion, because I was so happy to see him again." She asked me if that sounded crazy, since she'd never met him before.

I asked how he'd acted toward her. She told me that he looked startled and asked if they'd ever met—that she'd seemed familiar to him too. "We went out for coffee and talked like old friends. Ken mentioned he worked with boats. When I heard him say 'boats,' a feeling of fear and loneliness overwhelmed me. It was weird. I felt like I was living a situation I'd lived before," she added.

Connie had given Ken her phone number. They made plans to meet the following weekend. I was able to give her a past-life reading, "You experienced a definite déjà vu. The two of you did meet before—in a past life. In that life he left you and went to sea. Just remember, this happened already. So don't act toward Ken as if you think he will leave you. Time will tell the exact direction your relationship will take in this life. I predict you will stay together."

This session with Connie was over two years ago. Recently she returned, and I was happy to see that she and Ken were a couple. They were getting married and going on a honeymoon cruise together.

Jack Walks the Walk

My friend Jack, an actor, has talked extensively about his déjà vu experiences. "I was always obsessed with anything that related to New York City. I grew up in Denver and never felt comfortable living there. I'd watch movies that took place in New York, and every scene was totally familiar to me. My sister remembers that at the age of six I could describe parts of New York as if I lived there.

"I finally moved to New York fifteen years ago. I was very happy and felt as if now my life had finally begun. I met a man, Steve, who became my lover. I was meeting him for brunch for our first date. I remember watching him cross the street to meet me in front of the restaurant. A shock went through me, because I was so sure I knew him. We sat at a table and started talking. Everything about him was familiar—the way he laughed, held a cup, moved his hair off his forehead, and especially the way he walked. I've always been very aware of people's walks. I'd imitate certain walks: John Wayne, Charlie Chaplin, Jimmy Cagney.

A person's walk was unforgettable for me. Steve was a complex person, temperamental, moody, yet kind. A lot of people didn't understand him but I did from our first meeting. I just knew him.

"Steve became ill a few months after our first date. I was afraid and talked to my sister about the situation. I knew that it would be difficult, but I also felt it was my karma to take care of him. Somewhere in my subconscious I felt that Steve had cared for me in some other life. We'd been brought back together in order to balance our relationship. I loved him very much, but it was more involved than what appeared on the surface."

Steve died a few months after I first met Jack. I was able to give Jack a past-life reading concerning his relationship with Steve.

Jack's déjà vu was very real. He and Steve had been together before. Steve had nursed Jack through the bubonic plague in twelfth century France. In that life Steve had injured his leg, so he walked with a certain stiffness. That was the beginning of Jack's deep awareness of the way people walk. Steve had risked his own life to stay and nurse Jack. Jack had stayed by Steve through his illness in this life. The overwhelming need to get to New York had dual purposes. Jack needed to balance his karma with Steve, and his professional karmic success centered around New York.

This past-life reading confirmed Jack's feelings about the depth of his relationship with Steve. His need to be in New York didn't stem from his having lived in the city in a past life. Jack's current needs were presented to him in New York. He misses Steve every day. Yet he is grateful for the opportunity he'd been given to help his beloved friend.

EXERCISE: EXAMINE YOUR PERSONAL DÉJÀ VU

Thinking about your personal déjà vu experiences can give you a better understanding of reincarnation. This exercise can be a helpful instrument in shaping your present life.

Sit quietly and try to remember a time when you felt you already knew a person the very first time you'd met him or her. Think about this person and try to re-create the relationship.

How did you meet and where? What feelings surfaced? How did this relationship affect you? Was it a short-term relationship, or are you still in contact with the person? Did it have a happy or an ugly ending? Did you take more time with the person as a result of your déjà vu feeling? Did the relationship teach you a valuable lesson?

Now do the same mental examination and direct your thoughts to places you've been. What made you feel you'd been there before? Are you drawn to certain places? Are there places you're afraid to visit—or places that immediately frightened you when you did visit them? Take your time doing this déjà vu examination. Sometimes you will remember these feelings immediately, and other times you will remember them later.

Déjà vu experiences aren't always happy, and all feelings of familiarity—good or bad—aren't direct results from past-life situations. But since many of them are, recalling any personal déjà vu memories can help us in our quest to understand and believe in reincarnation. Try to do this often, because it takes time to unlock memories that are hidden in our subconscious minds.

Take out a *white* index card and write:

Be patient. It takes time to unlock memories that are hidden in our subconscious minds.

Whenever you have a few free minutes, sit quietly and see if you can remember people, places, feelings, or sensations that could signal a déjà vu. This will help a great deal in your ability to understand the continuity of life. It will also point out the impact past-life issues can have on our present-life situations.

It isn't necessary that we remember our past lives in order to live beautiful, useful, happy present ones. What *is* essential is that we live in the moment with love and integrity. We will see the results of our present actions during the rest of this life. We are shaping our futures by our current behavior. Let us always keep our minds open to receive the gift of knowledge.

We must never use past-life karma as an excuse for our lack of judgment in our present life. Here's a useful tip to jot down on a *white* index card:

Always reflect on your present-life patterns before delving into the realms of past-life possibilities.

A WORD ABOUT PAST-LIFE REGRESSION THERAPY

There is a current rage for past-life regression sessions. In these sessions the patient is hypnotized or relaxed and guided back to a time or place he may have lived before. This type of therapy can prove helpful when done by a trained psychic or therapist. The synthesis of the psychological and metaphysical can be a powerful healing method. There are many phobias and other traumas that are based not in this life but in a past one.

I believe that under hypnosis certain people are able to tap in to the Akashic records. This doesn't imply that these people can read into the Akasha at will. They are in a relaxed, trancelike state, and certain obscured past-life memories surface. This is very rare, but it can happen. If a person receives accurate past-life information, the effect will be seen in the present life. This knowledge should greatly serve to resolve a current trauma, phobia, or obsession.

Take out a *white* index card and write:

If a person receives accurate past-life information, the effect will be seen in the present one.

There are some excellent psychiatrists helping patients through past-life regression therapy. These doctors are very courageous. Most doctors are terrified that they will be ostracized by their peers if they dare to proclaim publicly that they believe in reincarnation or psychic phenomena. The lack of scientific proof stands as the main excuse for dismissing anything "paranormal."

Yet healthy skepticism isn't a bad thing. Nearly all past-life readings are *not* accurate. I've had at least fifty clients tell me they know they are living their last incarnation. They all have the same basis for this belief: They found it out during a past-life regression session. These people are usually unhappy with one or more of the following: work, love life, family, or money. Many suffer from depression and despair. What serious professional could tell these people that they'd achieved total self-mastery? Not only is it untrue, but it's also unkind. The best way I know of to find a reputable past-life regressionist is through the referral of someone you respect who's had a session. Another route would be through a book or an article written by, or about, a regressionist that gives practical and in-depth information about the work.

It's common sense that what we are in this life depends on how we acted in our past lives and how we are behaving in this one. So make certain if you have a past-life reading that you study the information and see how it helps you live more wisely in the here and now.

COLLECTIVE KARMA

The laws of reincarnation and karma must be applied to nations and races as well as to individuals. A nation is made up of a group of people constrained by politics, culture, and karma. It's quite simple to see differences among an Italian, a Frenchman, a Japanese, and an American. Language, traditions, and tastes vary a great deal. The karma of a nation is made up of the combined karma of all the people living in it. That is, each of us is born at a certain time into a certain country, race, and religion.

Lawrence once told me, "The modern revival in all areas of the metaphysical has a great deal to do with the many souls from the ancient civilizations of Egypt and Greece being born into our Western world."

This isn't necessarily our last earthly incarnation, but most of us lived one of our many past lives in these civilizations.

We can't excuse ourselves from social responsibility. We must do whatever we can to help the world around us. Any nation or empire built on injustice will sooner or later collapse. No action of service toward another is unimportant. We must ask ourselves if it's a person's karma to be hungry or if it is our karma to feed that person. Are we to allow ourselves to live in isolation, ignoring other countries for the benefit of our wealth and power? If we do, each one of us will eventually be reborn into poverty and impotence.

We must not forget that new karma is being born every second. This should make us more sensitive to the needs of others. World tragedies are broadcast immediately via satellite to our televisions, radios, and computers. It is almost impossible to remain unaware of the plights and disasters that befall others. The world will move into balance only when we all have contributed in any way we can for the good of all humanity. There are no insignificant actions when we are helping others.

"Do unto others as you would have done unto yourself"

is a deeply profound statement about karma. Think about the magnitude of those words. All actions create reactions. We are all connected to each other by our universal karma. Whatever we do, or do not do, will be returned to us.

KARMA CLEANING

The Karma Bank has no place for erasures. What we have done can never be undone. We can acknowledge our errors and decide to remedy situations, but we can't change the past. This explains why lots of people feel that they never get a break in life. "I do everything that I can to be a good person, but I keep having nothing but problems." This mystery can be explained by knowing that we have to deal with issues from not only our present life but also from our past ones. The person who keeps living a good life no matter what pressures she faces is building good karma for the future. We don't always have to wait for our next life to earn the reward from good deeds. (For example, Charlene gave a subway token to a woman who said she'd forgotten her wallet. Two weeks later she forgot her money while buying coffee, and the man behind her in line paid for it.) This life can take a turn for the better in a moment.

The average life is a mix of deposits and withdrawals, fortunes and misfortunes. Anybody who tells you that he or she can show you how to get rid of all your past karma is a grifter, a con artist. A client told me she'd paid five thousand dollars to a "karma cleaner." I thought that she was joking, because this was so insane.

"Did the cleaner use Windex?" I asked.

"She said a lot of chants in a language I didn't understand," the girl told me.

"It could be called a karma con or a karma caper. There is no such thing as 'cleaning' away past karma. It's just practical that you will suffer if you made someone else suffer. You can learn and go forward in life creating new good karma. I'm sorry that you spent all that money for something that can't be done," I explained.

"This lady is famous, so she must know what she's doing," the client told me.

"The devil is famous, but that doesn't mean we should do what *he* says," I snapped.

The client got my message. She was able to see that this "karma cleaning" notion was absurd. She left that day sadder but wiser.

KARMA AND SUICIDE

Suicide is never preordained. It is always a choice made in the present incarnation. Often it is carried out in a moment of unbearable emotional distress or total hopelessness. For some it appears to be the only way out of their torment. Loved ones left behind suffer intense grief, as well as guilt, shock, and anger at the unnatural interruption of life.

Newspapers are full of stories about people from all walks of life who choose suicide thinking it will be an end to their pain. This phenomenon isn't limited to adults. Today an alarming number of teenagers and even young children are taking their lives. I was shocked to learn that suicides out-number homicides in our country.

Suicide is not acceptable. It is an act of violence against the soul. Someone who takes his physical life doesn't die. Instead, the spirit resides between the earth and spirit worlds until the time of its normal passing. Normal passing means the time that the body would have passed over if death hadn't been self-inflicted.

The only time that it is karmically correct to take your life is in order to protect a higher truth. This becomes an act of courage and selflessness, an act that is divinely protected. For instance, you are a resistance fighter and you are captured. You know that you will be tortured and forced to reveal the names of other freedom fighters. You take your life to pro-tect them, thus protecting the greater cause: freedom. This action isn't punished; it is revered.

Karma did not force you to join the resistance. This was a decision you made. Karma placed you in an environment that allowed you to make this choice. Thus, the outcome of your capture and your decision to end your life to save oth-ers wasn't predestined. This kind of honor and nobility is apparent in the words of Sydney Carton, who gave his life in order to save his friends: "It is a far, far better thing that I do than I have ever done; it is a far, far better rest that I go, than I have ever known" (in *A Tale of Two Cities*, by Charles Dickens). Sydney's suicide was motivated by the highest ideal: to save the life of his friend. In doing so, he also saved the lives of his friend's wife, daughter, and father, and he served his country. This act of selflessness was karmically acceptable.

Most people who commit suicide are not evil. They are depressed, hopeless; they lack courage or the vision to see that where there is life there is hope. Life has become so complex that the only hope for peace seems to be beyond the grave.

Take out a *white* index card and write:

Where there is life, there is hope.

People who believe in karma and reincarnation rarely kill themselves. This belief affirms that you don't die, so you can't kill yourself.

Take out a *white* index card and write:

You don't die, so you can't kill yourself.

Impact

Suicide is devastating to all whose lives it touches. Suicide knows no age, race, gender; its impact is felt by everyone. There are not always clear signals that someone is going to take his life. But sometimes the warning signals are blinking like neon signs, saying, "Help me! Help me! Help me!" We must try to be aware of other people's pain. In many cases we could help prevent people from taking their lives. We must show them there *are* alternatives to suicide. We take on terrible karma when we let someone kill himself if we could have acted to avert it.

Lawrence once told me, "The impulse to commit suicide is greater in those years of a person's life that are divisible by seven without a remainder." This statement was food for thought. Of the cases that I knew about from my work, almost all fell into one of those seven-year cycles. He didn't give me any further insight into why the sevens appear to be more vulnerable. He just told me that they were. It's prudent to watch these time periods with an added intensity.

There is a great difference between people who meet accidental death and those who take their lives because they are afraid to face the world or just don't want to do so. There are deaths that may on first inspection appear to be suicides but turn out not to have been intentional. For example, a man has been undergoing treatment for severe emotional problems. A good doctor prescribes a medication that should help him. Tragically, an abnormal reaction to this medication occurs. The patient kills himself. He was being treated by an excellent doctor and taking the prescribed amount of medication. His motivation was to get better. This action may not constitute suicide because the patient was trying to promote life.

People Who Commit Suicide Don't Go to Hell

Karma doesn't punish a person for self-murder, any more than a wave intentionally drowns a man. It's wrong and cruel to think that people who commit suicide automatically go to hell. The suicide will remain between the earth and spirit worlds until the time he would have "passed over" if he hadn't killed himself. This isn't hell, but it is uncomfortable to hear the sorrow of the people you have left behind. It's a kind of never-never land, once again proving that you can't kill yourself. Your spirit does not die. No matter how you die, death is like taking off a coat, burning the garment, and announcing that you're dead. The truth is, you no longer have the physical covering, the coat. But you're still alive. Boomerang! You thought you'd be dead, and you aren't.

People need to realize that in every life a certain amount of rain must fall. Poor health and fear of pain are common reasons for ending physical life. But if you end one life before its karma has played out, you'll have to go through the illness or pain in another life.

EUTHANASIA

This is a hot issue, because many people believe they have the right to end their own life or the suffering of their loved ones. But there is no mercy in mercy killing. I want people to think of the bigger picture. Once you have released the karma of the illness by dying a natural death, it's over. You will rest in peace and be reborn without this torture. Why chance a whole other life with this illness?

Lawrence has spoken about this to me with great passion. "It's often compassion that makes people believe that mercy killing is the right thing to do," he said. "But this compassion is misguided. Who has the right to choose life or death for anyone, including themselves? The law of karma is a very decisive judge in this matter. If it's your karma to have a difficult death, it must be faced, or it will be repeated in a new life. Suicides or assisted deaths aren't the end of suffering.

They are the beginning of a much greater pain: spiritual suffering."

KARMA HAS NO DEADLINE

The results of *all* actions will be returned to us—if not in this life, then in a future one. Death doesn't erase karma. It merely delays it. You will live as many lives as you need to in order to balance your karmic bankbook. You will reincarnate with all your credits and debits in your karma bank account exactly as you left them when you died. There's no need to rush, because the fat lady is not going to sing before you have mastered yourself. Karma has no deadline.

Take out a *white* index card and write:

Karma has no deadline.

3. Karma and Health

Medicine is much more an art than a science.

— PARACELSUS

Health is of inestimable value to everyone. Some diseases have natural causes, and others appear to have mysterious origins. Those with natural causes have their roots in our present life. Diseases with unexplainable origins (for example, no family history, no dietary, environmental, or psychological basis, and so on) are karmic. They are brought to this life from a past life. Once the karma is balanced, good health will be restored. Sometimes we must live with a physical problem our whole life, and other times it will be resolved while we have time to enjoy life without it. A karmic health problem doesn't necessarily have to last a whole life span. The problem will be with us until the karma is balanced.

Physical health provides one of the greatest examples of

the law of cause and effect. How many times have you got-ten a cold or the flu because you were completely exhausted? This could be due to mental or physical overexertion. The fact that you allowed yourself to get run-down resulted in your getting sick. The boomcrang was obvious.

Of course, the roots of all illness are not always so evident. Many times it takes a buildup of emotions before the body rebels. But your body will revolt if forced to live in a state of imbalance. There isn't a great mystery in this type of health problem.

A short period of self-examination should hit the nail on the head. "I knew I was going to get sick but I just couldn't slow down" is a mantra heard in most workplaces. You could have avoided this situation if you'd "listened" to your body and taken a break. Sometimes overwork, due to an obsession for perfection, can lead to ill health. This can be averted by lightening up on mental and physical activity. We need to respect our bodies *and* our minds in order to live with the harmony of greater health.

Take out a *blue* index card and write:

I will respect my body and my mind so that I can live with the harmony of greater health.

We need to respect the health of others by not infecting them with our contagious diseases. How often have you gotten sick at work because someone gave you the flu? It's not always avoidable, as symptoms don't always surface in time, and you give your problem to somebody else. But it's bad karma not to try your best never to infect another person.

Take out a *blue* index card and write:

> I will do my very best never to infect another person with any illness.

And then there are sexually transmitted diseases. A person who is aware that he or she is infected with one of these—herpes, AIDS, genital warts, and so on—has a moral responsibility to inform a potential partner before there is any physical contact.

A misunderstanding of karma can cause a serious boomerang. I was shocked when a client who had AIDS told me that if someone had sex with him, he didn't feel the need to tell the person he has this disease. He said, "Whatever happens to them is their karma." I asked him about his responsibility to alert the partner of the danger involved. He arrogantly dismissed the idea of personal responsibility by saying, "It's not my problem." I replied, "Oh, yes it is, my dear. It's comparable to committing murder." (I never saw him again but later heard that he had died.) In his next life he will suffer the same type of death that he caused in this one.

Some people believe that if it's a person's karma to suffer, we must not interfere. Does any good doctor leave a patient in agony if she is able to administer relief? Does any Good Samaritan come upon an injured person and not offer help? Let's not forget that if it's our karma to be put in a position to help, it's our duty to try to avert tragedy. If we have a contagious condition, we have a responsibility to admit it. It's not always easy to tell people about have certain health problems, but the karma of deception is a heavy one. There are some very nice people who have upsetting health issues.

Take out a *blue* index card and write:

The karma for deception is a heavy one.

Joyce Dumps Gary

Joyce arrived to see me in a state of depression. She had been engaged to marry a guy named Gary. When Joyce went to the doctor for her yearly checkup, she was amazed to learn that she had herpes. The doctor informed her that the only way she could have contracted it was from intimate relations. Her only lover was Gary, so she confronted him. At first he denied it, but ultimately he admitted that he'd had a one-night stand with someone who meant nothing to him. This must have been how he contracted this disease. Although he apologized repeatedly, Joyce broke up with him anyway. She told him she would never be able to trust him again. Gary paid a high price for a one-night stand. He lost a wonderful woman, and he gained a social disease. Boomerang!

After Joyce and I discussed this situation, she was able to say that she was grateful it wasn't worse. She was also thankful it had occurred *before* the wedding. It was a great shock on more than one level. It was a blow to find out that Gary could have done something so hurtful. And it was terrible to have herpes as a lifelong reminder of Gary's betrayal.

Joyce returned to see me a year after our first meeting. She was dating a new man. Joyce had told him about the herpes within two weeks of their first date. She'd had no intention of taking any chance of transmitting the disease, and no desire to be intimate with someone she'd just met. He's a great guy, and they are enjoying each other. I was delighted to tell her that I "saw" a wonderful future for them. Joyce's integrity created the new good karma of attracting an honorable boyfriend.

VITAL FORCE

We are all born with a certain amount of energy. This is also known as *vital force*. As we grow older, the supply diminishes and the body starts slowing down or, in many cases, breaking down. The avoidance of worry and fatigue will help keep the body charged with vital force for a longer, healthier period of life. A balanced amount of physical exercise is life-affirming and helps the body increase flexibility and strength. Excessive, compulsive exercise is a misuse of vital force and can cause the body to rebel and become weakened. Lawrence is vehement about this. He once told me, "My child, a spiritually developed person would never walk from one side of a room to the other without a good reason. He would not want to waste any vital force."

Take out a *blue* index card and write:

Excessive, compulsive exercise is a misuse of vital force.

Nancy Misuses Her Vital Force

Nancy exercised three to four hours per day. If she missed a day's workout, she became hysterical. She stressed to me that she just didn't feel right unless she had her daily dose of jogging, the StairMaster, and high-impact aerobics. I asked, "How do you have energy to do anything else?" She insisted that her exercise routine made her feel great and that it gave her lots of stamina. But she looked anorexic: all skin and bones. I was tempted to go into my kitchen and make her a sandwich. I could see that she'd had many injuries, a bandaged ankle, scars on her knees, but she kept exercising anyway.

"Nancy, what are you running from?" I asked.

Looking at me as if I were crazy, she replied, "Nothing."

"Nancy, you are given only a certain amount of vital energy in a lifetime. If you use it all up exercising, you'll suffer from a lack of energy in the second part of your life." (She was twenty-five years old.)

"I don't believe that," she said. She was adamant that she didn't feel well without her routine. I saw that she would collapse if she didn't slow down. She wouldn't listen.

Twelve months later she came to see me again. Nancy had passed out at work and been taken to the hospital suffering from complete exhaustion and malnutrition. Life had forced her to slow down and look at what she was doing to herself. She'd been hospitalized for more than a month. Nancy was scared enough by what had happened to change her behavior. She was now exercising forty minutes four times a week and watching her nutrition. She still had days when it was hard to control her desire to exercise more strenuously, but she was working hard to keep herself in balance.

"I didn't understand what you meant about using up all my vital force. But the shock of being hospitalized helped me to get it," Nancy told me.

"Better late than never, Nancy," I said.

"I feel better now that I don't work out all the time, and I have a lot more energy for other interests. I was missing out on a lot of life by spending so much time running. Thank you for helping me. It wasn't until I was in the hospital that your words of warning began to make total sense to me. You must have thought I was crazy the last time I was here," she said with tears in her eyes.

Nancy had learned that energy and vital force are not to be taken for granted. It was unfortunate that she had to be hospitalized in order to wake up and smell the coffee. There is an easier way to learn: "Common sense in all things," as my grandmother used to tell me. There's a great deal of wisdom in this simple adage. It could save a person a lot of heartbreak and energy in the long run.

Disposition plays a central role in the state of our health. Temper tantrums, constant irritability, anger, and hysteria have become the norm for a lot of folks. People go crazy, and their only excuse is that they couldn't help it. "That's just the way that I am." "I blow up and let all my feelings out." "It's my nature to be angry." I've heard these excuses too many times to count. It seems to me that a lot of people in our society think it's just fine to act like jerks.

The consequences of a bad disposition affect the body's

balance. It might take years to see the boomerang effect of this type of behavior, but you will see it. Every time we lose our cool and blow up, we are using valuable portions of our vital force. We are also breaking down the body and the nervous system. Stomach problems, rashes, hair loss, headaches, and back pain are a few common afflictions resulting from negative mental and emotional habits.

I think it would be beneficial to realize that we can improve our nature. We must first recognize aspects of nature that cause ourselves and others disharmony. Once this is acknowledged, with a little bit of true grit we can change our actions and reactions. The end result will be a healthier physical, mental, social, and spiritual life. And by this positive action, vital force is conserved.

Take out a *blue* index card and write this:

You are given only a certain amount of vital force in a lifetime. Don't waste it!

All sickness isn't rooted in bad disposition or a waste of vital force. But I can assure you that you'll never feel great as long as you allow yourself to live in a state of agitation. A common factor in the lives of many of my clients and much of humanity is a high level of anger, expressed in such questions as "Why me?" or "Why is it *my* karma that everything is so difficult?"

Karma must not be used as an excuse for bad temper and excessive behavior that results in ill health. Good health is most often the result of positive thinking and action. Before we blame a past life for our present health problem, we must examine this life and study our current lifestyle. People who break the natural laws of good health—eating poorly, drinking alcohol in excess, smoking cigarettes, not exercising, never getting adequate sleep, always being irritable and angry—are living in denial if they blame their illness on past-life karma.

Here is an exercise that will help determine if an illness is rooted in this life or a past one. Take out your *Power of Karma* Journal and begin.

EXERCISE: THE ROOT OF THE PROBLEM

1. Write down any health problem or issue you have: fatigue, allergies, skin problems, headaches, thinning hair or nails, weight fluctuations, a cold that won't clear up, swollen glands, bleeding gums, etc.

2. Carefully examine your list and be absolutely honest with yourself. Are any of these problems the result of current bad habits? Cigarette smoking, drinking excessive amounts of alcohol, or lack of proper diet and exercise can cause present-life problems. These problems are most often resolved through moderation, discipline, or abstinence. On the other hand, some symptoms can alert you to a larger problem that requires professional medical treatment. If you see that you are not attracting medical problems because of bad habits, and you can't find a basis in this life, it's karma. You brought the problem in from a past life. Remember, karma has no deadline. If you

abused your body by overindulgence in a past life and thought you got away with it—wrong! You will be given the problem to face in this incarnation, or a future one, until you can resolve it.

The bottom line is, no matter what the roots are, the problems must be dealt with in the here and now. We can take immediate action to improve our health.

When Illness Is a Blessing in Disguise

Diseases are not always disasters. They can be karmic wake-up calls.

Mitchell, a client of mine, worked seventy-hour weeks and suffered from migraine headaches and melancholia. His marriage was on the rocks because he had no time for his wife and daughter. He had no balance in his life. He slept very little, ate badly, and wouldn't listen to anyone who advised him to do otherwise. He'd been told by his wife, brother, mother, and a colleague that he was killing himself. But Mitchell continued living his unbalanced way.

He came to me for a consultation but was interested in hearing only about money and power. He was obsessed with making millions of dollars in the quickest possible way. I cautioned him about his health, pointing out that I saw life-threatening stomach problems. My warning fell on deaf ears. I told him his aura indicated that he was at a breaking point. He didn't want to hear about health problems. But he was intrigued by the aura and asked me to explain it to him.

THE AURA

An aura is an essence that emanates from people, animals, and things.

To most people, auras are invisible. Some people, like myself, are able to see auras. An aura is a psychic, cloudlike substance created by our thoughts. Each thought gives out a vibration, accompanied by a color. The colors and vibrations of our auras change with each thought produced. Thoughts that pass through our minds quickly don't create lasting forms. These can be referred to as "passing thoughts." Others, because of their intensity or repetition, will become powerful auras that can greatly affect our lives.

There are many shades of each color that denote different feelings or problems. Mitchell's aura was a deep, heavy, gray color; it surrounded him completely and alerted me to his depression and headaches. If the gray had been pale, I would have interpreted it as fear. As we spoke of his desire for great material success, a deep orange seeped into his aura. This particular shade of orange indicated excessive ambition. A lighter orange would denote a sense of pride. There was a bright red aura emanating from his stomach area, revealing his problems with ulcers.

Sometimes I see auras; other times I feel them. It's all a matter of being sensitive to vibration. A person must have psychic ability to see auras; it's a form of clairvoyance, not a sign of higher spiritual development. Many people who aren't very spiritual are known to have the ability to read auras.

The color and vibration of an aura are the direct result of the person's level of thinking and acting. The aura will emanate beauty, health, and harmony in direct proportion to the character of the person. The reverse is also true: envy, hatred, greed, jealousy, and all other forms of negativity will emanate from an aura. We can change the colors in our aura only by changing the nature of our thinking and behavior.

I finished my explanation about auras and proceeded to plead with Mitchell to go to his doctor for a complete physical. I suggested that he spend some time examining his lifestyle to help him see how out of balance he was. Mitchell simply wasn't ready to face facts: health, harmony, self-preservation, or balance. He was heading for serious trouble. There was nothing left for me to say. It was up to him to choose how to live his own life. I could not interfere with his karma. Six months later I heard he'd been rushed to the hospital with a bleeding ulcer. He very nearly died. It took close to a year of total rest, good nutrition, and lack of stress for him to recover.

Mitchell returned for a second session, a very different man. He said that his illness was a blessing in disguise, and as a result of it he was reshaping his life. He had resigned from his job and was working from home. He was doing just fine and was no longer obsessed with money. Mitchell was having a great time with his wife and daughter. The headaches, the depression, and the ulcer—direct results of stress—were gone.

Mitchell could have died, but he chose instead to change. He was now able to find greater health and joy in his life. He had to kill off the parts of himself that were causing him bad karma. He was doing a stellar job restructuring his lifestyle.

"How's my aura now?" he asked.

"It's a beautiful color of blue, a shade that shows a respect for the sacredness of life," I answered.

HATRED: A DANGEROUS EMOTION

Hatred is always detrimental to health. It just isn't possible to hate and be healthy at the same time. None of us is ever hurt as badly by what someone does to us as by our own negative reactions to an injury, and we must do everything we can to nip hatred in the bud. Patience and tolerance are two of the best weapons against hatred. A major cause of insanity is uncontrolled hatred or anger. Imagine our bodies as being wired (like a lamp). A buildup of negativity rooted in hate or anger can cause a short circuit.

Think about this: Does hatred ever solve any problem? Of course it doesn't. It only adds to our confusion and makes it more difficult for us to resolve conflicts.

"Focus on the solution instead of the problem," Lawrence has said repeatedly. Hatred always attracts negative karma. There is no place in a loving heart for any hatred. Nonetheless, there may be times when we carry feelings of hatred, yet we must do all we can to overcome it and restore karmic balance.

EXERCISE: OVERCOME HATRED

Sit quietly and make your mind focus on the object of your hatred. Look closely. Is this a person who has offended you? A boss who has humiliated you? A spouse or lover by whom you feel betrayed or abandoned? Are you feeling this emotion toward a family member or a friend?

Now that you have faced the problem, let's move toward finding a solution. Focus on letting go. Visualize your mind letting go of the hatred, like a hand opening to release confetti. Replace the words or thoughts of hate with phrases of forgiveness and understanding. You may find this difficult or impossible on the first few attempts. Don't give up! Maybe you can only hold on to the forgiveness thought for a few seconds, but do it. Do this contemplation exercise daily for forty days, and then forty more if you can. This is essential to your happiness and to mastering yourself. Hatred must go! The good karma of great health can't be reaped in a field of hatred.

Take out two *blue* index cards and write:

1. Focus on the solution instead of the problem.
2. Hatred is always detrimental to health.

CLEAR-CUT CASES OF PAST-LIFE KARMA

Any physical problem is the working out of karma, be it rooted in this life or in a previous one. The great test is how we deal with the problem.

Take out a *blue* index card and write:

Any physical problem is the working out of karma rooted in this life or a past life.

Barbara: A Profile of Integrity

Barbara was born with one arm much shorter than the other. She's a beautiful woman with a strong, lean body, thick, beautiful hair, lovely facial features, and a highly developed sense of humor and style. It takes only a few minutes before you forget about her damaged arm, as her overall physical and spiritual beauty obscures the imperfection. But the fact remains, she's stuck with a deformed right arm.

Barbara's mother had a normal pregnancy—she neither smoked nor drank alcohol or caffeine; she didn't even take aspirin. Barbara's parents are still happily married, and they have three other children who were born with no physical defects. When she was a child, Barbara's parents took her to all kinds of doctors, and she struggled through numerous painful therapies and treatments. At the age of twelve she asked her parents to stop trying to fix her arm. She decided to find the best way to live with the problem.

"Kids are cruel," she told me. They made fun of her, and

it hurt a lot. But Barbara refused to allow anyone to destroy her sense of dignity. Her family treated her well, but she knew they had great difficulty dealing with her imperfection. Her father withdrew because he didn't know how to cope with his feelings of guilt. Her mother never treated her like a girl with a problem, and thus refused to acknowledge some of the problems Barbara faced. Her siblings had various reactions, ranging from sadness to jealousy. One sister felt that Barb got more attention because of her deformity. In time Barbara's example helped both her parents and her siblings. The bottom line is that Barbara knew she couldn't change the length of her limb. She could only control how she handled the problem.

I helped her by explaining how past-life problems can be brought into our present life. Her deformity could not be explained by present-life circumstances. It had to be a karmic situation resulting from behavior in a previous one. This philosophy made total sense to Barbara. Even though she couldn't remember her past lives, she didn't feel cheated or treated unfairly by life. Rather, she accepted her current-life test as the result of a prior-life action. Barbara is engaged to a nice guy who never even notices her arm. She is studying art history and business. Barb jokes about her amazing ability to type with one hand. She's also very aware that many people have much worse deformities.

Barbara stands as a shining example of a person who has accepted her problem and made a beautiful life in spite of it. She is shaping her future in this life, as well as her future lives. Her ability to deal with her karmic problem is balancing the out-of-balance karma she was born with. She will not be reborn with a deformity. Barbara's positive living is creating new good karma every minute.

Luke: Only the Good Die Young

Luke died of cancer as I was writing this book. He was a vital thirty-two-year-old, happily married to my friend Dee, and the father of two sons ages five and almost two.

Last May I received a call from Dee telling me that she had some bad news. Luke had been suffering from back pain. He'd gone for massages and had seen a chiropractor. When the pain persisted, he went to see his general practitioner, who initially felt there was no reason to be alarmed. Just four months earlier Luke had started a great new job. He'd had a thorough physical exam for life insurance purposes and was given a clean bill of health.

Luke's doctor was concerned by his pain level and ordered a series of tests. The results we not only shocking but tragic. Luke, a nonsmoker, had some rare form of lung cancer. It had spread throughout his body like wildfire. There were so many tumors in his body that it was impossible to remove them without leaving him paralyzed. The back pain was a result of the cancer pressing against his spine.

How could this have happened? Life was good for this family. Luke had recently received his M.B.A. and was thrilled with his new position at a great firm. Dee, a very successful writer, was looking forward to Luke's being able to spend more time with the family, now that he had graduated from business school.

Dee gave me this news with a combination of disbelief,

fear, and a firm conviction to fight for Luke's life. We dis-cussed the treatment options. Lawrence had told me about a tea made from a special plant that had helped people with tumors. I got some of this tea to Dee, who ran it by Luke's doctors; they had no problem with it. (I never prescribe any kind of medical treatments. I insisted that Dee make sure this tea was okay with the medical team.)

Luke drank the tea three time per day as he underwent chemotherapy and radiation. Later, after Luke had passed on, Dee thanked me for the tea.

It had helped her and Luke feel they were doing some-thing to promote health even as the medical reports wors-ened. She was amazing throughout this tragedy. Luke fought his disease with courage, love, and humor. He lived only six months after the initial diagnosis.

There can be no doubt that this illness was a clear-cut case of karma. Luke had fulfilled his earthly duty and was released from the physical plane. He is now residing in the spirit world in a state of perfect harmony. He will be waiting for Dee, his sons, his friends, and his family when it is their turn to pass over. Remember, we reside in the spirit world from eight hundred to twelve hundred years before our souls are ready to be reborn into another earthly incarnation.

As the Greeks said so beautifully, "Only the good die young." This wasn't meant to be a depressing statement, as many people have misinterpreted it. The Greeks felt that physical death was the ultimate gift for a soul. Death was the door prize, not the booby prize. Dee is living with the mem-ory of her husband's greatness of soul. She's very sad, yet secure in the fact that she did everything humanly possible to help Luke live until he died. She's not only courageous but a shining example of a person who has put her beliefs into action.

I'm asked over and over what to do if a situation seems impossible to cope with.

Take out a *blue* index card and write:

I will deal with this test minute by minute.

KARMA AND ADDICTIONS

I've had many clients tell me that a family member stopped an addiction—smoking, alcohol, drugs, or another harmful, excessive habit—then died of an illness related to the addiction anyway. It's very important to understand that we must conquer any addictions while we are on earth. Doing so frees us from having to be reborn with the same addiction. Once the dependence is conquered, we are freed from the bad karma of that particular abusive behavior. We don't have to go through the painful withdrawal ever again! Good karma is created the moment the addiction is overcome. It's never too late!

An addiction is a compulsive, uncontrolled habit. We are all fighting to overcome some type of addiction, whether it's of a chemical nature (drugs, alcohol, caffeine, or sugar), or some other type of compulsion (gambling, cleaning, watching television, exercising, shopping, overeating, the Internet, or sex). Addictions of any kind destroy the balance of our physical, emotional, and spiritual life. They steal our freedom. It's terrible when we "need" to have something as opposed to choosing to partake of it. Have you ever seen the torment of a person who is having a nicotine fit, a caffeine headache, or a drug-withdrawal symptom, or fighting the urge to take a drink? It's horrible for the person in need. The people watching can do little but be supportive and sympathetic. It creates good karma to be kind and firm with someone who is fighting to overcome an addiction. You can send positive thoughts to give the sufferer strength and reap the positive benefits that come from serving a person in trouble. It may be difficult to divert the addicted person from the object of his desire, but the bitterest medicine is often the most effective.

There are many theories concerning the root of addictions. Some experts believe they are inherited. For example, we know that certain people are born with a physical dependence on chemical substances, passed in utero from the mother. Environment has also been shown to be a significant factor in forming an addictive personality. If you don't overcome an addiction in a past life, you'll be born with the tendency to overindulge again.

I've observed hundreds of clients with addictions—resulting both from this life and from past-life karma. Many have had the tendency run throughout their family, and just as many have not. I know a family with five sons. Two of the boys are alcoholics, and the other three aren't. Their father drank a bit when he was in the navy, but he never became a drunk. He has no desire to drink more than an occasional beer. The mother doesn't enjoy drinking and has maybe a couple of drinks a year at a social gathering. The boys were loved, and the parents did everything to help the two alcoholic sons recover. In this family there doesn't appear to be either a physical or psychological basis for the addictions. Never forget that we are creating new karma, not just living out past karma. These boys developed their addiction in this life, and they will have to fight to overcome it. They were known as party animals, and the drinking was, and to a degree still is, a symptom of immaturity.

As of this moment one son has been sober for five years. The other boy knows he has a problem but hasn't found the strength to overcome it. His family remains helpful but aware that he must find the strength to stop himself; nobody can do it for him. I know that if he keeps trying to find a way to quit, he will do so. The key is that we must never stop fighting to overcome any addiction that steals our freedom.

"Any addiction or disease is rooted in violent passion. Any such passion—be it hatred, anger, lust, revenge, selfishness, or greed—affects the constitution of the person," Lawrence told me. "These extreme emotions act on the body's vital force, causing the body's energy to flow chaotically. This breaks the natural flow of energy that promotes health. We must not despair, because it is possible to conquer our addictions and passions—and live with greater health in this life and in our next lives."

Though it takes a strong will and a great deal of discipline, we can learn to control the imbalance, thus gaining a feeling of greater health and energy.

Take out a *blue* index card and write:

If I don't overcome my addiction in this life, I will be born with it in the next one.

THE USE OF THE WILL

Many people have been taught to believe that a person can do anything that he wants as long as he has enough *will* to accomplish it. Nothing could be further from the truth. There is a common delusion that willpower is a substitute for trained ability.

Yes, will is an essential factor in any type of change or recovery, but it must be combined with proper action. How cruel it is when we accuse people of having no willpower to overcome an addiction. Let's take cigarette smoking for an example. I know many people who have tried over and over to stop smoking; my own mother died from smoking-related issues. She had tried many times to quit, but she just couldn't. This didn't make her a weak or bad person, just a human being with an insurmountable problem to overcome. Mother was able to stop for periods of time, but the urge to smoke would be too difficult to resist, and before long she'd pick up the habit again.

The important thing is that she tried. She will be given other chances to break this addiction when she is reincarnated. Her karmic bank account will have a *need to stop smoking* listed in the deficits column. Mother will be reborn, and she will take up the cigarette habit again (or whatever form of "cigarette" habit exists at the time she is reborn). She will try again to quit, and sooner or later she will win the battle over this addiction.

All problems must be resolved while we are living in the physical world. Once we have conquered a destructive habit, we won't have to go through the pain of having to break the habit again in another life. Simply put, we won't be born with the desire to overindulge.

We've all met people who have never smoked, drunk alcohol in excess, taken medication unless absolutely necessary, or been intemperate with food, sex, shopping, or any other common excessive behaviors. This doesn't mean that they are "better" than others. It indicates that they overcame their individual addictions in another life, or that they have other problems to deal with.

It's true that Mother would have had a longer life if she hadn't continued to smoke. When Mother was dying, Lawrence told me that her habit wasn't from a past life. It was initiated by the stresses of this one.

I can vouch for the difficulty in quitting cigarettes. It took me at least seven attempts before I was able to defeat the dragon nicotine. I'm happy to say that I quit almost twenty years ago; I never desire to smoke now. I smoked because I was very sensitive, and it seemed to calm me down. In retrospect, that wasn't the best way to deal with sensitivity. (I'm certain that my habit was not a past-life one. I've read my Akashic records, and I hadn't smoked in any prior incarnation.)

It was extremely hard at first, but, like all difficult things, it got easier as time passed. I share this with you because it seems impossible to quit addictions when we are under their control. Also, it is seems impossible to envision the future without our "friends" the cigarettes, the drugs, the booze, or the unhealthy foods.

"Don't go negative. There is no chance to break bad habits unless you remain positive, productive, and kind to yourself and others. You must desire to stop something with all your might, or there is almost no chance of quitting. That indeed involves the use of the will. So, yes, the will can be strengthened, and this power greatly assists us as we fight to control our addictions," Lawrence has stressed.

We can't always recognize an addiction without some introspection. For example, some people think that their drinking isn't an addiction because they drink only beer and wine, not hard liquor. They ignore the fact that they get drunk a lot and cause pain to themselves and their loved ones. Others may think that they don't have a drug problem because they "only" smoke pot—every day. They don't do heroin or cocaine, but they are potheads, and it's illegal. Pot is a drug that keeps them in a fog, unable to have the energy to fulfill their dreams. They can't stop smoking it. They can't or won't admit it's an addiction.

Take out your *Power of Karma* Journal:

1. Write down any tendency you have to overindulge in addictive things: alcohol, drugs, food, sex, cigarettes, gambling, the need to control, to name a few.

2. Every day for seven days note how these problems are affecting your life. Be honest. Just a few sentences at the end of each day will tell you if you are in control of

yourself or not. (If you are too hungover, high, or coughing too hard to hold a pen to write, you are out of balance big time.)

3. On the eighth day read what you have written over the past week. Do you notice any pattern? It should be clear if you have an addiction. Interestingly, most people do have some form of addiction.

4. Make a list of what you'd like to quit. Now you should be ready to decide which is the most important addiction to overcome at this point in your life. *Underline it!* Do not try to force yourself to tackle more than one challenge at a time. You will defeat yourself if you make things too difficult. At this point you must begin to act upon your decision.

Seven is the number that is known as the source of all change. In this exercise, seven days should be the proper time you need to face the fact that you have a problem.

Take out two *blue* index cards and write:

1. The power of the will lies in my individual skill in directing it.

2. Every day I will focus on my goal and fight for it.

You must make a personal commitment to overcome any addiction. There are many ways to overcome addictions. You may need medical help as you withdraw from certain substances. A cold turkey could become a dead turkey if you don't release toxic substances in the proper way. A support group or a wise friend and a firm resolve are paramount as you fight for your freedom. You must let go of your ego and become humble as you face the fact that you have an addiction. Remember, we are linking our past lives to the present and the present to the future. The good karma reaped from ridding yourself of any addiction carries on from life to life.

Our ultimate goal is to relish the rest of this life and our next ones. We need to be objective and look at our good and bad traits without a filter. It will be difficult at first, but day by day, little by little, it will become easier. Don't despair. If your first attempt fails, pick yourself up and start again. You will win the battle if you remain tenacious. Think of all the great karma that you will acquire as you become liberated.

Take out a *blue* index card and write:

My ultimate goal is to live so that I can relish this life and the next ones as a better person.

KARMA AND CARBOHYDRATES

It may surprise you to hear that three out of ten clients ask me if I can predict when they will lose weight. They also ask if it's their karma never to be thin. Some people ask these questions jokingly, and others are dead serious. I have heard the heartbreak of people who struggle with their desire to shed the ten unwanted pounds and the despair of the dangerously obese. We live in a society that is very overweight and, at the same time, diet- and exercise-obsessed. It becomes a vicious cycle for many, from losing to gaining to finally giving up.

People can be unkind about other people's weight. Schoolchildren call their overweight peers "fatty," "porker," or "pig." These barbs stay with people the rest of their lives and can result in low self-esteem, depression, and various eating disorders. Adults can be brutal, refusing to hire the overweight, making cruel jokes, or just acting as if overweight people don't exist.

Every person who doesn't have a weight problem should be kind to those who do. Some people have a karmic weight problem because they abused their bodies in a past life or were unkind to others who weren't thin. That's a boomerang.

Not all weight problems stem from overindulgence or eating the wrong foods. Predisposition to a certain body type and metabolism can be karmic. One can be born with health issues that can affect weight, such as diabetes, or joint problems that make exercise difficult. But if you desire to lose weight, whether you have a karmic problem or not, it's wise to stop making excuses for your lack of self-discipline. I stress this because it creates bad karma to complain about something that you *can* control.

People *can* reshape their physical bodies. It may be very difficult, but what of value comes easily? Dieting can be a drag. Exercise can be torture unless we change our point of view from one of deprivation to one of integration. When we feel deprived, anger and self-pity result. Integration, on the other hand, means that the joy we receive from achieving our goals replaces any negative feelings. We are happy to do whatever we must in order to realize our dreams. It becomes easy to stop doing things that make us unhappy!

Take out a *blue* index card and write:

I will change my point of view from one of deprivation to one of integration.

David's Karmic Conflict

Here is an example of a mistaken karmic reason for obesity. When I met with David, he weighed three hundred pounds and seldom left his apartment. In fact, it was only sheer desperation that got him out to meet with me. He had zero self-esteem and was severely depressed.

"David, I see that you have great talent as a painter" were the first words out of my mouth.

"How could you know that?" He looked surprised.

"Aren't you here today because you're interested in my psychic ability to see things about you without being told?" I laughed as I said this.

"Yes, that's exactly why I'm here," he answered. "May I ask you a question?"

"Of course, I'm here to help in any way that I'm able to. Every person has many issues to deal with. It's not possible in one session to handle everything. I want to deal with the issues that are the most important to you, David," I explained.

"Why is it my karma to never lose weight? Every morning I wake up and tell myself I will stay on a diet. I do fine for three or four days. In fact, I almost starve myself, and then I break down and eat everything in sight. After I do this, I become so depressed I eat more and more." He started to cry.

"David, can you tell me why you are so angry with your mother?" I asked.

He looked up through his tears and said, "I hate her. She was always telling me how fat I was and that she was ashamed to be seen with me. Watching everything that I put in my mouth, she would yell if I ate anything she thought was fattening. I wasn't that big, but my mother had a skinny obsession. I don't think she ever weighed more than one hundred ten pounds, and she was five foot five. I became an expert at sneaking food."

"David, it isn't your karma never to be thin. It is your karma to have the mother that you do. Don't confuse your karma," I said with a smile.

"You don't think that I chose my mother on purpose?" he asked in a shocked tone.

"David, there is no chance involved in the birth process. We have the parents that we do because of past-life connections. Maybe you treated your mother in a past-life the way she treated you in this one. Hamlet said, 'There are more things in heaven and earth, Horatio, Than are dreamt of in your philosophy.' "

"You mean that things are not always as they appear?" David asked.

"Precisely," I answered. "I'm not saying that your mother's behavior was correct, but you need to let go of the past. She's no longer standing over you—you are in control of what you put into your mouth. I realize that you are trying to get back at your mother by overeating, but you're only harming yourself. Don't waste your sacred energy by remaining angry at your mother. This energy could be used in positive ways."

"What kinds of ways?" He perked up as he asked this.

"David, you could kill two birds with one stone. You could lose weight, and you could give the world a chance to enjoy your art." I paused in order to let him respond. He sat there as if in a state of contemplation. I waited a minute, then added, "It's easier to stop overeating than it is to continue living in your self-imposed prison, David."

"Do you really see that I can lose the weight and become a successful artist? How do I start again? I always fail," he said with a touch of self-pity.

"David, I think you're a terrific person and a very talented artist. You have been given the karmic test of dealing with a difficult mother. Most people think their mothers are difficult in one way or another. Think about the good things in your life, and that will help you to begin a new program toward health and harmony. Start in small ways. No one can starve himself for three days and not overreact by eating too much. It's just too hard. We usually walk before we run, don't we?" I asked.

We talked more about his mother. "I don't really hate her, but I am very angry with her. It helps me to hear that she and I have past-life karma. I never understood why she was so hard on me. There was nothing in this life that could explain her behavior. She was so kind to others, and she never yelled at my dad. This gives me some real food for thought," he added.

"You can feed your thoughts with as much positive energy as you can give them. But stop blaming karma for your current lack of discipline," I said with humor.

David agreed to buy a *Power of Karma* Journal and to keep a record of his food intake. I also told him to start a walking program—forty minutes of slow walking three days a week. He could increase this when he felt that he'd enjoy more exercise. He was to record his walking to support his new diet, physical and mental. But first he was to get a medical checkup!

I told him it would take great patience and commitment, as well as learning to love himself, if he were to take the weight off and keep it off. And he'd have to use understanding in order to forgive his mother. These virtues could be learned by taking life moment by moment. A year after our meeting, David called. He'd lost sixty pounds and felt like a new person.

His mother still made him angry sometimes, but he didn't allow these negative feelings to interfere with his life. Occasionally he slipped and ate too much for the wrong reasons. He accepted these setbacks and was able to get back on the right track swiftly.

"I have a painting I'd like to send you," he said. "My work is going great, and I love painting again." After David hung up, I thought, *He finally is freed from the wrong idea of karma.* David had taken responsibility for his own actions and was enjoying his life minute by minute. He had learned that although we are born into our families because of past-life karma, it is our free choice how we deal with them in the present moment. He would now carry this knowledge through the rest of his life and into the next ones. He would find that he balanced the karma with his mother and wouldn't have to deal with this type of trauma again. His call had made my day.

Sparta

One day Lawrence talked to me about perfection. "The modern-day overemphasis on the perfection of the physical body is directly connected to the fact that there are many people alive today who once lived in ancient Sparta. Not all Greek cities had the same life philosophies. Sparta was partly a gym and partly a training camp for hand-to-hand combat. The citizens were always in training. The complete social view was shaped by breeding and raising a strong, beautiful race. Deformed infants were put to death. A wife was expected not only to produce athletes but to build her own muscles and compete in sports as well. The greatest part of Spartans' lives was spent in achieving perfect bodies. To be the most beautiful man in Sparta was the height of human ecstasy. A criminal could get off with his life if he were beautiful. It would have been considered sinful to put an end to such a creature. Think about the number of statues that still remain from this period in history, each one glorifying the perfection of the nude male body."

This made complete sense to me as I considered Lawrence's statement. Think about it: marathon races, gymnasiums on every corner, spas, body building and sculpting, boxing, and the Olympic Games certainly parallel our modern world with that of ancient Sparta. Most of today's fashion decisions are made by designers prejudiced against the female form. Women are trying to look like body builders or young boys in order to fit into the current fashions. And people who are not in good physical shape are treated, in many cases, like social outcasts, even though one out of three people is overweight! Nudity is everywhere—movies, magazines, television, the Internet.

"A penny for your thoughts," Lawrence interjected.

"You always give me amazing insights and reasons for many things. But isn't that a rather one-sided view of the Greeks? You've spoken to me in the past about the Athenian way of life, and it was very different," I said.

"My child, all cities are not alike. It's like comparing New York City to Boston. Athens and Sparta had a great deal of social differences. The Athenians had gymnastic habits, for they respected a healthy body, but not to the extent of the Spartans. The Athenians also spent much of their leisure time listening to philosophers such as Plato. The Athenians had greater balance."

Love your body as the divine instrument that houses the soul. This will keep you from being plagued with feelings of despair because your body isn't perfect. Too much time is consumed by thinking about losing weight: High protein? No carbohydrates? Only carbohydrates? Liquids? Counting calories? No fat? Sugar-free? Fruit only? You must understand that this overemphasis on the physical will cause a boomerang effect. You mustn't obsess about your body instead of gracefully approaching the proper mode of diet and exercise. I guarantee you'll never lose and maintain the proper body weight if you keep on obsessing. You'll also create bad karma by living in a constant state of negativity.

To be consumed with the shape of the physical body can lead to depression, despair, and disharmony. The Spartans lived a "spartan" lifestyle—they ate well and moderately, and lived frugally. Though obsessed with their bodies, their lifestyle did not foster eating disorders. Anorexia, bulimia, binge eating, and excessive exercise are all symptoms of living immoderately. A healthy body is attained through a combination of proper feeding, moving, and thinking. It takes self-discipline to attain any of our goals, weight or otherwise. But everything must begin with a proper point of view.

Helen Changes Her Body and Her Point of View

A client named Helen came to see me for the third time. Her previous session had been a year earlier. It took me a minute to recognize her. She was thirty pounds thinner, dressed to kill, and had the aura of a happy woman. "Helen, you look great. No offense, but you seem like a different person," I commented.

"Do you remember the last time I was here?" she asked.

"I seem to recall that you were complaining about your inability to lose weight. You were feeling depressed and had negative feelings, and you got very angry with me," I replied.

"You told me to stop feeling sorry for myself, because I didn't have any problems that couldn't be solved," she said with a laugh.

"Looks like you took the advice," I said.

"I left your place that day feeling that you had been insensitive to my needs. You stressed that I had to change my point of view in order to change any part of my life, body or otherwise. You told me to wake up each morning and spend a few minutes thinking about all the things that I had to be grateful for. You reiterated that I must stop complaining about things that I had the power to change. Because I'd attract real trouble by my lack of gratitude. That advice seemed corny and not psychic enough, but something compelled me to try." She smiled.

"Helen, did you expect me to tell you to light a candle, wear a crystal necklace, or buy a magic carpet?" I joked.

"Something like that," she said.

Helen had worked hard to transform her thoughts from ones of self-pity to ones charged with positive action. Slowly but surely, her life began to turn around. Previously, dieting had always been very difficult, but this time, after a few months, it wasn't. Helen started thinking about what she could do to be good to her body instead of constantly being angry that she had to cut out foods that put on excess weight. Every morning she spent important minutes reflecting on reasons for gratitude.

It wasn't just Helen's weight loss that was obvious; it was the negativity she'd shed that made the greatest difference in her appearance. As she was leaving that day, she vowed to keep her point of view in shape. "Gratitude is magic," Helen said as she walked toward the elevator.

"You got that right, Helen," I added as the elevator doors closed.

Lawrence and I had a long discussion about self-discipline.

"Lawrence," I asked, "since self-discipline doesn't come naturally to most people, can you suggest ways to make it easier? I have some trouble with the concept of discipline, because it implies force. True integration doesn't demand force, because you *want* to do whatever is needed to achieve the desired goal."

Lawrence sat back in his chair and smiled. "My child," he said, "you sound so grave!"

I was forced to laugh at myself. He was right. I relaxed and listened.

"Any major undertaking requires discipline. A great musician or artist lives a life of amazing discipline. But look at the results! Why should it be different for someone to create the body she would love to have?

"People often rebel against any type of discipline, because it reminds them of their childhood. At those times they were forced to do their homework or eat their vegetables, perhaps, when they'd rather have been playing or eating candy. They feel it limits their freedom. Simple but true.

"Many people are children living in adult bodies. Look at it this way: If you are used to eating only candy, for a while you may have to use discipline to eat a balanced diet. In time, as your tastes change and you have more energy, you will not crave the food that is not good for you. You will automatically prefer good, healthy food. Discipline, in this case, has served you well and led you to become integrated. This is what you are striving for. When this happens, you are free. The desire for the fattening foods is no longer there. With true integration there is no need for force.

"Discipline should never be equated with perfectionism. Merely do the very best that you can, and be satisfied that you are developing at your own rate. Do not become angry with yourself every time you start toward a goal and fail to meet your own expectations. Accept your mistakes and shortcomings with gratitude for the opportunity to learn from them. To agonize over your shortcomings is a form of negativity and will create bad karma. You have heard the saying that 'self-pity stinks.' It does. Let go and move forward."

We sat together in silence, and then Lawrence spoke again. "Life is a series of breaking bad habits. Habits die hard. The destructive ones must be replaced with constructive ones. If you remove an old habit without replacing it with a new good one, you will feel an emptiness, a hollowness, where the old habit once was. People must look toward their desired goal with joy and enthusiasm, not like it's a stone around the neck. It all begins and ends with love. Love being the best person you can be. Enjoy the journey, not just the destination."

Here are some useful tools to help you achieve the shape you want your body to be in. Take out your *Power of Karma* Journal.

1. Write down everything that you eat, no matter how small the amount.
2. Promise yourself that you will do this every day for forty days. Remember, the number forty has a powerful psychic force. It is the number of completion.

3. Examine the list to determine why your body is not in balance.

4. Decide that you will follow a healthy, lower-calorie diet for forty days. Again, write everything down. You will see the change in your journal and in the mirror.

4. Karma and Sex

Sex is a potent force of nature. It can be a creator or a destroyer. Sex is not only a physical instinct but also a complex, mystical, and deeply enigmatic one. It creates life, expresses love, and can ignite beauty and creativity. Sex can express the purest spiritual union between two souls. The result of this union is a sense of connection, of two people feeling as if they were one.

Many people, through the sexual act, try to renew their connection with the God force, the higher self within them. Life has become so overly consumed by the physical needs of daily existence that we have forgotten the spiritual. We often feel lost, empty, and alone. Through this powerful and immediate feeling of total union with another person, we feel a sort of abnormal amount of connection that approximates our forgotten sense of unity with the God force.

Sex as a release from our feelings of separation is wonderful if love and trust are involved. Sex can be a teacher. We can learn to love on an intimate, spiritual level. It takes consideration, sensitivity, and patience to develop a balanced sexual relationship. On the other hand, when sex is used to exploit, manipulate, control, terrorize, or for purely selfish gratification, the result is often disconnection, rage, loneliness, and despair. It can also put us in potentially life-threatening states of disease.

Sex can be a trap. Many people become irrational when they are intensely sexually attracted to someone. You can try to warn them to take more time, but such warnings usually fall upon deaf ears. Doesn't it stand to reason that until you meet the right person, who has proved his or her character, you should just wait? This is common sense, but judgment falls by the wayside when one becomes enraptured by attraction to another.

MOONSTRUCK

Jill came to see me in a state bordering on hysteria. She was in love with Tim and could think of nothing but her beloved. However, there were a few problems: Jill had a husband, and Tim had a wife. Each had two children. But all Jill kept repeating was "I've never had sex like this. It's unbelievable. Tim and I are crazy about each other. We are insanely in love. I can't eat or sleep. I live for the time we have together."

"Jill, how would you feel if you discovered your husband having a torrid affair?" I asked.

"I'd feel awful, but what can I do? This just happened

between Tim and me. We weren't looking for this. It must be our karma," she replied.

"Jill, everything is karma," I explained. "I think you believe that your relationship with Tim was predestined."

"Wasn't it?" she asked.

"No, you were destined to be tested," I answered. "There was and is free choice in the midst of our desires. It's human that you were attracted to each other. It was your own decision to act upon that attraction. Don't misinterpret karma or blame destiny for your personal choice to have an affair with Tim."

"It's not an affair," Jill snapped.

"Jill, what would you call it at this point?" I asked. "You and Tim have known each other for less than a month and have had sex three times."

"How do you know that?" she gruffly retorted. Jill was silent for a moment, then spoke a bit more civilly. "I forgot I was talking to a psychic. But the word 'affair' doesn't express our love."

"Would you feel better if I called it an affair of the heart?" I asked her.

"It's very spiritual between us," she added.

"Jill, I'm afraid your passion has knocked out your judgment. Passion can be spiritual when combined with respect and knowledge of each other's character. That type of relationship takes time to build. You simply haven't had enough time to get to know each other. And you must think about how your behavior can affect others."

I looked at Jill and saw a great deal of trouble around the

corner if she continued on this path. Her husband would find out, divorce her, and fight to gain full custody of the children. Tim wouldn't leave his wife, and she'd be very sorry that she hadn't handled things differently. I tried to tell her this as kindly as possible. My words fell on deaf ears. Jill got angry at me and protested, "You must be wrong. It's true love, and we can't control ourselves."

I told her that she still had time to avert the trouble that would come from this mess. She should stop seeing Tim until they both had separated from their spouses. This could be done with dignity and integrity. Time would tell if they were meant to be together. Jill said, "Are you crazy? What if he finds someone else while I'm trying to do things slower?"

"I thought you told me that it was true love? Aren't you confusing love for lust?" I asked.

"No!" she snapped.

I brought up the karma between Jill and her husband and Tim and his wife. She did not want to hear about personal responsibility. "Jill, what do you want me to do? Lie to you? You came here for my psychic reading on this situation. I've told you what I see happening and that you are not destiny's victim. There are choices that can be made that will ensure a better outcome. Can't you think about the bigger picture? You'll never be happy if you make others suffer unnecessarily by your selfishness. It can happen that two people fall in love when they aren't free. But true love won't vanish because two people act responsibly and respectfully toward the other parties involved. On the other hand, sexual attraction can disappear as quickly as it started if it's not rooted in a stable relationship."

"What do you mean by 'stable'?" Jill asked.

"There's an old Chinese saying: 'Don't judge the house by its paint,' " I answered.

"I don't get it," she replied.

"The house may have a beautiful exterior, but its foundation may not be solid. A sensible person would spend some time examining the total house before buying it. A foolish person would say he doesn't care about what's not immediately visible. He loves the paint job, so he buys it without further investigation. Time reveals there are lots of problems with the house. People, like houses, must be given an opportunity to prove they are solid, and that takes time."

Jill started to cry and said, "Why can't I just have some fun? I work hard and take care of the house and kids. I love having sex with Tim, and he loves me. I've never had great sex with my husband. I didn't know how miserable I was until I met Tim."

"Is it fun deceiving your husband and Tim's wife? Can't you just take the stardust out of your eyes and realize that you must behave in harmony with the law of karma or it will boomerang back upon you?"

"What do you mean?" Jill asked through her tears.

I quoted what Lawrence had told me: "It is easy to be kind and gentle to our mates as long as we are in love with them. People who can be in love with someone else but still act in a loving, respectful manner toward their mate have learned to behave in harmony with the law of karma."

"Jill, it's quite simple. There is a lesson to be learned from all this. You will save yourself a lot of heartbreak if you take care of your responsibilities at home and *then* see how things go with Tim. I know that you believe you're in love and that it's overwhelming and unbalancing. Don't destroy any future happiness by allowing sexual passion to override all sense of judgment."

I took a deep breath and looked at Jill. She was still moonstruck. She was out of her mind with her desire for Tim. She had to execute her free choice in dealing with this situation. I'd done what I felt I could to help her avert a tragedy. Jill would reap good karma if she acted with integrity and kindness toward all parties. This would be difficult, near to impossible in her current state. She would sow the bad karma that results from selfish, irresponsible behavior if she acted only upon her desire for immediate gratification. Time would tell.

BOOMERANG

Jill returned a few months later. She looked awful. The first words out of her mouth were "I guess you're going to say 'I told you so.' "

"Listen, toots," I told her, "I'm not your mother or your conscience. Do you think I like seeing people unhappy and depressed? I tried to warn you that you were cruising for a bruising. After that, it's your life to live in any way you decide to live it."

Jill said that she was sorry and that she wasn't mad at me; she was angry at herself. She related what had occurred since we'd last met. Her husband had found out everything. He noticed that Jill was acting as if she was hiding something. He asked her if she was having an affair, and Jill denied it emphatically. He didn't believe her and hired a detective to follow her.

The detective knew the exact amount of time Jill had spent with Tim and the hotels they'd been in. These details, with pictures of Tim and Jill going in and out of hotels, were given to her husband. Jill's husband didn't tell her that he knew about the affair and let it go on for a month before he nailed her with all the evidence.

In her state of shock she could do nothing but admit everything. Her husband became irrational and called her every name in the book. The kids were home and heard their parents fighting. Jill started to cry, yet she kept telling her husband that she was sorry but she was in love. Her husband then proceeded to call Tim's wife and tell her everything. She'd had no idea that her husband was having an affair, and she subsequently had a nervous breakdown. Jill's husband would reap the bad karma for his act of revenge. Two wrongs never make a right. He should never have called Tim's wife because of his anger.

Tim told Jill he didn't want to see her anymore because it was "too much trouble." He refused to see her, to answer her phone calls, or to return E-mails. One of Tim's coworkers told Jill that Tim and his wife had decided to patch things up.

Jill's husband, enraged and humiliated, filed for divorce. He wanted Jill out of the house and demanded full custody of the children. Jill hired an attorney, all the while pleading with her husband for another chance. I was not surprised this had happened, but I was a bit shocked that it had occurred so fast.

Boomerang. Jill's action caused her husband's reaction.

Tim had never been in love with Jill, and he had turned out to be weak and selfish. Jill was now in a big mess, one that could have been avoided if she'd taken time to get to know Tim before she got involved with him.

"What was I thinking?" Jill asked.

"You weren't thinking; you were acting as if you'd been beguiled. Sex was a trap for you, and this is the result. Nobody could have made you listen, because you were not acting rationally. You must take a harsh look at your life and discover what is at the root of your self-destructive tendencies."

"What can I do to fix this problem with my husband?" Jill asked. I told her to take out two *pink* index cards and write:

1. Passion without a firm foundation delivers a heavy punch to our judgment.
2. I will act with the highest principles of unselfishness. Only this can save my marriage from the state it has fallen into.

I also told Jill to buy a *Power of Karma* Journal and to:

1. Write an honest record of everything that has happened. Study it.
2. Face the music. You can't change the past, but you can learn from it.
3. List the good things that are still in your life and be grateful for them.

These tools will help her as she tries to mend fences with her husband.

Jill and her husband are still living under the same roof, but things are far from harmonious. She's paying the price for her behavior. Her husband is only tolerating her until he can find a way out. What goes around does come around— not always this rapidly, but it will one way or another. The lesson is this: Had Jill exercised patience and integrity, she would have seen that Tim wasn't Prince Charming, would have avoided heartbreak and scandal, and would have kept her husband. And that being moonstruck is a choice, not a karmic situation.

DEBBIE TURNS TRAGEDY INTO FARCE

In a state of near nervous collapse, a woman named Debbie came to see me. It seemed she had met a young European man who was visiting America and had fallen madly in love. After knowing him for three weeks, she left the States and moved to France to be with her beloved. Everyone who cared about her tried to tell her she should take more time before changing her life so drastically. But she allowed her passion to overrule her judgment. Within a few days she began to see that he had a rather unusual behavior pattern. He disappeared for hours at a time with no explanation, and when he finally returned, he was cold and distant.

Debbie had taken all of her savings with her, and, knowing that she didn't speak French, her beloved had offered to open up a bank account for her. After waiting two days for his return, she became hysterical, imagining all the horrible things that might have happened to him. She finally went to a small bar they had visited a few times. She approached the owner and told him that her boyfriend had disappeared. The owner began to laugh. He said, "I hope you didn't give him any money. He's nothing but a gigolo." Suddenly she realized that she had been betrayed. She was left with nothing to do but call her family and ask them to send her money to buy a ticket home.

Debbie could have avoided this whole terrible situation, if she had only waited to get to know this guy. Her sexual attraction had clouded her reason. She came to me because she wanted me to tell her that she had been the victim of karma. I told her that I was afraid her misfortune was a definite case of bad judgment and sexual attraction.

"You mustn't *blame* karma for your own foolishness. If you had exercised even a minute amount of patience and self-discipline, you could have avoided a great deal of suffering. In the long run, Debbie, it is all a part of experience, and it is all right," I said. "Learn from this situation and get on with your life. Time is a great healer, and it will serve you well."

I told her to write this statement on a *pink* index card:

Karma has no victims.

I also told her to take out her *Power of Karma* Journal and:

1. List all the people who had warned her not to go to Paris with this loser.
2. Record the reasons they had given her not to act rashly.
3. Look at these two lists and study them well. This will

help her in the future to know whom to discuss dilemmas with.

4. List all the good karma in her life: her family, friends, the fact that she hadn't been physically hurt and had suffered only a bruised ego, to name a few.

This exercise would help her to put her victim fantasy into perspective. Debbie thanked me for helping her.

"Maybe you should put 'learn French' on your to-do list," I joked.

"Are you kidding? I can't even look at a French fry," she said, and then started to chuckle. After a moment she added, "I haven't had a good laugh since this affair started."

"Debbie, laughter is one of the greatest remedies for stress. It gives the nervous system a rest, and it feels good. Humor is a lost art for many people. There's rarely a situation that doesn't have a humorous side. You were seeing your love affair as a Greek tragedy, and now you have turned it into a French farce. How clever you are." I laughed as well.

She left that day with a smile on her face and a firm decision not to let history repeat itself. She was indeed no victim! Debbie's karma would remain balanced if she continued to "look before she leaped."

FALLING IN LOVE WITH SEX ISN'T ALWAYS FALLING IN LOVE

Let's face it, everyone in the world wants to feel "in love." If we are honest, we must admit that we're afraid of being lonely.

When we think about being "in" love, we think of being joined to another person on an intimate, deep, and complete level. The result of this union is a feeling of exhilaration and excitement. It's like nothing else in the world. We believe that this relationship will heal our wounds, make us feel safe, desired, and loved. Of course, we also believe that it will last forever. However, if this relationship ends, depression, anger, and the desire to get even are common reactions. It's difficult to admit to ourselves that we entered into a relationship because of physical attraction alone. Sexual attraction can be immediate, but love takes time, because it involves learning.

Karen Has a Safe Landing

On a recent flight back to New York from Paris, a flight attendant named Karen shared her story of one broken affair after another. Karen was aware of repeating the same pattern of behavior over and over. She admitted to having sexual affairs before she'd had time to discover the true character of her lovers.

She said her deepest desire was to be married and have children. I pointed out that she was sabotaging herself by repeating actions that weren't leading her to her desired goal. "But I love sex! It's the only time I feel totally alive!" she insisted.

Karen was in conflict between her desire for sexual gratification and her need for the deep union that can come with marriage and children. Karen felt completely alive only when she was having a sexual affair because for that brief time she felt a deep link with another person. Since she hadn't taken time to build a firm foundation, the relationships based solely on sexual attraction ended. Karen had no idea that she was subconsciously desperate to feel the connection to the God force within.

"There's nothing wrong with enjoying sex, but you should think before you act if you want to attract a committed relationship," I told her.

"How can I find someone who will give me both good sex and security?" she wanted to know.

I explained the good karma of being patient and getting to know someone and assured her that she could earn what she was looking for. "Karen, I'm going to give you some exercises to help you stop picking losers," I said.

Karen whined that she had no discipline, so she couldn't do any exercises that were difficult or time-consuming. I told her, "Fine with me, but don't waste my time asking for advice if you're not willing to take it. Karen, you should take a minute to *think*. You have no ability to be objective in your love life. I'm sure you carry this negative trait into all aspects of your life. Your lack of gratitude for my trying to help you shows an amazing degree of narcissism. Most people would find it difficult to love someone who is so self-consumed."

Karen looked a bit stunned at my rebuke, but she came back with an impressive amount of moxie. "Give me those exercises," she said, then added, "please."

I replied, "Write this down on a *pink* index card. Memorize it—and do it."

I vow that under no circumstances will I become intimate with anyone I meet until after an absolute minimum of forty days.

I was surprised when Karen said, "I can do that."

"Karen," I said, "buy a journal and label it *Power of Karma*. I'm going to give you a very important exercise that you must do in order to develop your judgment skills." (I gave Karen and Paula the same exercises, so I'll share Paula's story and then give the exercise at the end.)

Paula Is Trapped by Sex

Paula married a man whom she had known for only two months. Having been totally swept off her feet, she would listen to no one who advised her to wait. Her friends were concerned and begged her not to rush into the marriage. They arranged for her to have an appointment with me before the wedding. I also advised against the marriage. I told her I saw that this man was a liar and was sleeping with other women. I went so far as to tell Paula the name of one of the other women. But even worse, I saw that he was mentally unbalanced and had a dangerous violent streak. I feared he would hurt her. Paula seemed mesmerized by her attraction to her intended. Nothing I said had any effect on her decision. "Sex can be a trap," I told Paula.

"What do you mean?" she snapped.

"Well, it doesn't take a rocket scientist to know that your sex life with this guy is affecting your judgment. Sex can be wonderful and beautiful, but it can also cause people to try to make a silk purse out of a sow's ear." Asking her questions about her beau, I found she knew nothing about his past. Over and over she would repeat that she knew he loved her and that she'd never had sex like this before.

I felt bad for Paula when she left the session, because I knew that she was in for serious trouble. Yet, on the other hand, I knew that I couldn't stop the karmic boomerang. It was her life. I can only do my best to advise someone; following that, it's up to the individual to do as he or she sees fit.

Six weeks later Paula returned. It's highly unusual for me to allow anyone to return for a session that soon, because I don't advocate dependency, and my psychic predictions usually won't change dramatically in that short a period of time. But Paula needed clarification. She had been married for twenty-one days. On their wedding night Paula's husband had started yelling at her and calling her a whore. Through her tears she told me that his language was too disgusting to repeat. He tore her underwear to shreds in his crazed fury. Terrified, Paula ran out of the hotel room wearing only a towel. The management called the police, and Paula was given a tranquilizer by the hotel doctor.

She moved back to her parents' home for her protection and hired a lawyer to arrange an annulment. This man kept calling, threatening to kill her. As unbelievable as this situation may seem, unfortunately, I've seen it too many times. "Mary," Paula asked between her sobs, "how can I avoid this in the future?"

"Paula, from now on you must learn to *do your homework*. It's wonderful to meet a person you're attracted to, but once the relationship is established, you must then begin the hard work. Attraction is usually instantaneous; getting to know the person takes time. The only way to discern the character of a person is through observation, experience, and history, all of which take time." The art of discernment is perfected like any other great expertise—ballet dancing, painting, playing music—through repetition and discipline.

I told Paula to buy a *Power of Karma* Journal and index cards. Following is the exercise I gave her—and Karen.

EXERCISE: LEARNING DISCERNMENT

Once in a blue moon I have clients who are definitely intuitive, and I tell them to follow their gut feelings. Their personal history has proven their intuition to be accurate. But that is not the norm. Like Karen and Paula, over the years hundreds of people have come to me in grief, despair, or humiliation because once again they've become intimate with someone they did not know. Their consistent, tragic flaw was that they trusted their first, gut instinct. *Boomerang!* How much heartbreak could have been avoided if only they'd waited?

Take out your *Power of Karma* Journal. Accounts of experiences written as close as possible to the time they occur are the most accurate history.

1. Record your *very first* impression of anyone you feel you might become intimately involved with. Date it.
2. Write in the journal (and on a *pink* index card that you always keep with you): *No intimate involvement for a minimum period of forty days.* (If a person tries to push you, dump that person immediately. This is a neon sign telling

you that you are being disrespected. Disrespect always creates negative karma.)

3. Record the progress of the relationship—just a few lines daily. Nothing too time-consuming. Always remember: common sense in all things, including karma. (Does he call when he says he's going to call? Confirm plans? Does she want to meet your friends? Relatives? Does she want to introduce you to her loved ones? Where did you go? What did you share? How easy is it to talk to each other?)

4. Be thrilled if you can write down that the person you like is scrutinizing you in the same way. It indicates someone who is looking for love in all the right places. Just as you are.

5. At the end of forty days, if your relationship is not over, then your instinct might pass the test of time. The karma is still undecided, so proceed with dignity, integrity, and cautious optimism.

6. At the end of forty days, if your relationship is over, you must be totally honest with yourself. Read what you recorded. It may hurt or embarrass you, but at least you have the facts in front of you. History does not have to repeat itself. Changing your history changes your karma.

Eight months later Karen called and reported she'd done her exercises faithfully. With great pride she said, "I've been dating a wonderful guy for four months. He says he wants a future with me."

Paula is still single. The threatening phone calls have stopped. She continues to do her homework. She is happy to wait until she meets a man with character.

Judy's New Rage

Judy came to see me in a fit of anger, demanding that I tell her where she would meet the man of her dreams. Bored of dating and tired of being alone, she sought solace and help in finding her true love. She had a terrible chip on her shoulder because of her unhappy childhood. I told her that in my point of view she must heal her childhood in order to be free enough to attract a mate. She didn't like this message. She was expecting to be given psychic directions to her rendezvous with the perfect man.

Going on, I explained how her low self-esteem was affecting her ability to attract a good man. I gave Judy a detailed account of her childhood. Her father had abandoned the family when she was seven, and her mother had gone into a depression. Judy had never understood why her dad left, so she'd felt responsible. Her mother wasn't capable of giving her daughter any affection, compliments, or encouragement. This resulted in Judy's feeling angry and confused. Her aura burned with rage. And her past was putting up roadblocks to achieving a healthy, balanced present. Judy was stunned that I came up with this much psychic information. She sat silently, tears running down her cheeks. "What can I do?' she asked through her sobs.

I gave Judy a *pink* index card and told her to write:

The past can't be changed, but I can alter the way I let it affect me in the present.

I then explained a meditation practice that I knew would help her free herself from the prison of her anger:

Building self-worth: Sit in a quiet place where you will not be interrupted. Spend a few minutes envisioning yourself happy. Don't put another person into the picture. Just see yourself leaving your home with a joyful look on your face and a bounce in your step. The day is beautiful, and you don't have a worry in the world. Hold that picture for as long as you can. Do this exercise twice a day. Remember, don't put anyone else into the picture. You are feeling great because you're alive and it's a beautiful day. You feel terrific just because you're you. Do this short meditation for forty days in a row. After the forty days you can decide to continue or not. The change within you will most likely make you want to continue. Short periods of meditation that you do often can be more potent than forcing yourself to meditate for an hour.

I told Judy about the *Power of Karma* Journal and told her to get one and write:

The things I like about myself.

Don't go negative. Nobody is perfect. Just list the good stuff, be it nice teeth, healthy hair, pretty hands, a great sense of color, love of animals, or that you're always on time, kind to people, ready to lend a helping hand. Add to the list whenever you think of another positive aspect. Review this list frequently. Enjoy being able to add to it. This will help you to have a realistic view of your positive attributes, and self-esteem will follow.

Then I gave Judy an exercise, to do when she felt ready.

EXERCISE ON FORGIVENESS

"I want you to forgive your father for leaving and forgive your mother for being weak. You don't have to approve of their behavior, but you must try to put yourself in their shoes. Remember, what is done is done. So let's work at letting go of the past and building a beautiful future." Then I stopped talking.

"How do I do that?" she asked.

"Take a few minutes every day to see yourself observing your parents in a very objective way," I counseled. "Send them loving thoughts. Realize they're human beings with their own karma to deal with. As you breathe, feel your anger release through your breath. Your anger toward them is boomeranging back upon yourself. It's keeping you from attracting balanced, loving relationships into your life. Next, see yourself feeling good about your parents. That may seem hard at first, but work at it. In time you will realize that your anger has dissipated, and you will begin to attract beautiful people into your life. Don't put yourself on a schedule; just take things hour by hour, day by day."

KARMIC CONNECTIONS

Later I explained to Judy that each of us has parents who are determined by past-life experience, as related to me by Lawrence:

"Mankind must understand the karmic connections that affect our lives. Everyone we become close to in this life has had a relationship with us in a past incarnation. The soul of your mother in this life may have been your daughter in a past one. Your current husband may have been your brother, sister, parent, or child. There are no accidents of birth. We have our parents, siblings, race, citizenship, sex—all because these elements are our karmic inheritance. But karma must never be an excuse for our problems. A woman who keeps choosing immature men who cannot commit to a relationship should not confuse karma for lack of wisdom. Instead, she should look within herself and see why she keeps repeating the same pattern. Once she recognizes the problem, the solution can come swiftly. This process of self-examination is priceless as we keep working toward balance in all our relationships."

Judy returned to see me a year later. She was dating a really great fellow named Matt, and was on cloud nine. She'd met him one afternoon as she was sitting in a café, writing in her journal. Matt struck up a conversation with her, and they've been dating ever since. She's released her anger toward her parents, which has made her feel like a new person. Judy continues to do her exercises, but it's easy for her to envision herself happier—because she is.

Judy is no longer living in denial and confusion about her

childhood. Cynical people would say that it's not possible to stop living in the past until one has spent years talking about it. That isn't true. Sometimes going over and over something we can't change only causes us grief and depression. Any positive action we perform will enhance our present situation and produce the good karma that comes from love and forgiveness. Talking about the past can be healing; beating it to death without coming to terms with it is destructive. We can face the issues that cause us disharmony, thus promoting greater balance in our lives. But at a certain point it becomes destructive, because it destroys our peace of mind. It stops us from enjoying the present and the future. It keeps us in a constant state of boomerang! Over and over we keep bringing our anger back upon ourselves. The simple meditation outlined above will help more than you can imagine. Just try, and the results will be clear.

Just Stop

Lawrence came to my apartment one evening, and we had a long talk about the grave implications of living in the past. "The past is a series of memories. We can change the way we feel about our memories as we change our point of view. My child, you must help people to see the negative results of living in the past. This can lead to nothing but despair and, if taken too far, imbalance or insanity. One of the major causes of people's lack of joy lies in their relentless demand to be unhappy because of past injustices. This is comparable to a dog chasing its tail. I believe that most often the antidote for this malady is just to stop, whenever you see yourself allowing the mind to dwell on the past. Stop, breathe deeply, and think of a beautiful image. A sunset, the sea, a mountaintop, a laughing child, a crackling fire in a hearth—anything that you choose. The mind can hold only one thought at a time. It's a bit like the alchemist who transmuted cheap metal into gold. The past image of injustice can be replaced by a present beauty. Simple, yes, but very effective. Try it!"

KARMA AND THE ZEBRA'S STRIPES

"I know that if I help him, he will be able to change." "She just needs my love, and she'll be able to overcome her drinking problem." "Oh, I know that Tony sleeps around and always has. But I believe him when he says he loves me and will now for the first time be totally faithful to one woman. He's a completely different person when we're together." "I know that for twenty years Bill has never been able to keep a job for more than a few months, but with my constant love I'm sure this time he'll be able to keep this new job." "Sarah just thinks that she's a lesbian. She needs to experience true love with a man like me."

These are just a few examples of what I've heard, time and time again, from my clients over the years. People believe they can change another person's makeup. I say, snap out of it! You *cannot* change the zebra stripes that make up a person's constitution. The distinctive qualities of the individual soul can be altered only by the person him- or herself. It never hurts to try to help people, but it's judgmental to decide what is better for someone else. And it's egotistical, and useless to believe you can or should alter anybody. We all can alter our own bad habits, and others can support us in the process. But there is a critical difference between habits and traits. Traits are "zebra stripes" that define a person's character. They are tattoos that can't be removed without a skin graft.

How to Recognize a Zebra's Stripe

An inborn trait, or a zebra's stripe, is behavior that has been consistent in a person since a young age:

- habitual lying, even when there seems to be no reason for it
- never keeping promises
- need for a number of sexual partners, even when involved in a happy personal relationship
- need for secrecy
- addictions that interfere with good reason
- no real remorse, no matter how many times another person has been hurt
- inability to keep employment
- sexual orientation

For example, if a person tells you she's gay, she's gay. There is nothing wrong with being gay; it can be an essential part of someone's makeup. By the same token, if you think someone is gay, and she tells you she is straight, it's not your "karmic duty" to help her come out. If a person tells you he has never been faithful to a lover, believe him. If someone says he doesn't want to stop excessive drinking, he doesn't!

KARMA AND KUNDALINI

Kundalini is the Sanskrit word for the Hindu concept of the serpentlike force that rests at the base of the spine. This force moves up the spine and discharges itself in different ways. It can be set free through the purely physical act of sexual relations. It can be liberated as an expression of tenderness, or through the medium of artistic accomplishment. Love, creativity, and spiritual aspirations allow this often dormant energy to release itself in harmony with nature.

We can learn to channel our kundalini energy into creative expressions, not by suppression but though redirection. If properly channeled, it becomes creative, such as with music, art, or poetry. If misused, it can cause a person to become unbalanced; an example of this would be preoccupation with sexual desire and overemphasis on one's lower nature. Human beings are composed of a physical self and a spiritual self. The spiritual self is also known as the higher body. The physical represents the lower nature. We have a choice as to how we channel this sacred energy. If the mind is focused on love, beauty, and serving others, the kundalini will flow in a beautiful, harmonious way.

Lawrence spoke to me about sex and energy. "The sexual instinct is rooted in man's fear of loneliness. The kundalini force is a passionate, creative fire burning within each one of us. Misuse of this force has caused mankind to become overly involved with sexual desire. Many frustrated people are not doing their true creative work and thus find themselves having meaningless sexual encounters. These sexual affairs allow the life energy that is bottled up inside to be released, but the lack of love leaves people feeling empty. Depression is often a result of the misguided kundalini energy used in these encounters. This emptiness and despair can bring nothing but bad karma, because valuable life force is wasted. People must learn to channel this energy so that the effect will be love and balance in life and work. This redirection of energy will bring good karma, because it will be used for creation."

He continued, "When two spiritually minded souls fall in love, there is a rich blending of soul and body. Sex as mere recreation must be reevaluated. We are being warned by the prevalence of sexual diseases that an imbalance has been created. Instant gratification is just that: a mere momentary thrill. Then what? People are left to look at themselves. Everyone has a choice as to how to channel the energy that is within. Will it become creative energy used, for example, in true loving relationships, music, art, writing, or service to others? Or will it be wasted on preoccupation with sexual desire and an overemphasis on man's lower nature?" He stopped talking and waited for me to respond.

I told Lawrence that I was intrigued by the number of people who were coming to talk to me about their sex-related problems. I felt that many of them were confused because they thought sex was the root of their unhappiness. The real underlying issue was that people wanted to contribute whatever abilities they had to the world at large. They were only half alive, so the sex act made them feel whole for a moment and quickly empty again—a vicious cycle. I felt that the explanation of kundalini would help many people to start living a fuller life, a life rooted in creative work and deep relationships. "Sex can be beautiful when it is the expression of deep love," Lawrence said, ending our conversation. As I sat thinking about this, my friend James's story came to my mind.

James, Talent, and Kundalini

I first met James during the summer of 1989 while on vacation in a small resort town on Cape Cod. I was with a group of friends, and we stopped at a piano bar to hear him play. He was quite well known, so the place was packed. James appeared to be around thirty, handsome in a boyish way, with an easygoing charm. Stools surrounded his grand piano, and a number of women were vying for the seats closest to James. He paid attention to all the regulars, playing their requests and chatting between numbers.

I'd studied music for many years and had been a professional singer, so I know a lot about music. James started a set of show tunes and standards, then broke out and played "Rhapsody on a Theme of Paganini" by Rachmaninoff, followed by Brahms's "Intermezzo," and ended with one of the best renditions of Gershwin's "Rhapsody in Blue" I'd ever heard. I was stunned by the magnitude of his talent.

When James took a break, we were introduced. I liked him immediately, and we made a date for lunch. We quickly became friends, and he told me he'd gotten a master's degree in music from Juilliard. His dream had been to be a classical pianist and composer. He'd graduated, played concerts in small halls outside New York for about a year, and was then offered the piano bar gig in Cape Cod. James took it because he was tired, desperate for a steady income, and he intended to stay for only six months. It was now seven years since he'd taken the job. I immediately sensed that he was very sad because he wasn't following his true talent and passion, classical music. At the same time I saw that he was upset with himself because he kept having a series of empty sexual encounters.

When I told James what I saw, he was a bit stunned. "You hit it on the nose," he said. He revealed that the only time he felt a bit better was when he was making love. This act made him feel alive for the moment, but immediately afterward he felt empty and selfish. He didn't want to hurt people, but he couldn't seem to stop himself from having these one-night stands.

I said, as gently as possible, "James, you're burning up inside because you aren't channeling your true creative force. This suppressed creativity is looking for a voice. What you really desire is the powerful connection that creativity brings to you—the feeling of being connected to the God force within you. You're confused, so you're searching in the wrong direction. You keep having sexual encounters that hold little or no meaning for you because, for that moment, you feel connected. It's a temporary connection, so at the end you are left sadder than ever."

James started to cry. My words had hit home. From that day on, James promised himself to make a conscious effort to change his life. He would concentrate on channeling his energy into creative works. He wanted to try to find a woman to whom he was attracted but who also shared his passion for music. It's been twelve years since James and I became friends. He's had three compositions published and performed them in the United States and Europe. James is deeply in love with a young woman. He describes her as his best friend, greatest fan, and only lover.

"It wasn't an easy journey, but what a hoot. It just keeps getting better and better," he told me when we last talked. James is very grateful for everything, including his sanity. He now understands the power of directing sex and energy into creativity and true love.

Take out a *pink* index card and write:

Kundalini energy follows the direction of thought. Think beauty, harmony, balance, and service, and the road will be crystal clear.

Keep this card in your pocket, use it for a bookmark, or frame it on your desk. Don't forget, the kundalini energy can be unbalancing if not focused in the proper direction. It's not a toy to be played with. It's a sacred force that can bring us vitality and creativity. Simply put: Waste not, want not.

KARMIC RELATIONSHIPS

Sexual attraction is very intense, but without an emotional link it can cause confusion. People may think they are in love, but, too often, time reveals that what they felt wasn't love but physical attraction. However, when sex is connected with love, it is not only a physical but also a spiritual relationship. It is the merging of souls.

There is karma, past and present, linked to this kind of love. We have been involved in a relationship with our beloved in a past life. This subconscious connection adds to the overall stability of the relationship. We feel that we know a person more than it seems that we should. Of course, not all past-life connections bring joy and harmony. Sometimes we are paying a karmic debt. For example, maybe you betrayed a soul in a past life, and now it seems that you are being betrayed. You must first examine your behavior in this life before you try to figure out if you are reaping karma from a past life.

DO WE HAVE A SOUL MATE?

The desire to unite with another person in a committed romantic love relationship is one of the deepest needs each human is born with. Ninety percent of all my clients desire to know how, when, or if they have found their true love. The term usually used to describe this one-on-one personal love relationship is "soul mate." The truth is, there's no such thing as a soul mate.

I would like to share a conversation on the subject of soul mates that I had with Lawrence. I received a message from Lawrence to go Edgartown on Martha's Vineyard. It was the third time he'd chosen that area for a meeting. It was off-season, so the island was quiet, and I had no trouble booking my favorite room at the Daggett House.

Lawrence asked me to meet him at a beautiful garden called My Toi on Chappaquiddick, a short ferry ride from Edgartown. As usual, we talked about many things. At one point during our conversation the concept of soul mates arose. Here is what he had to say on that subject:

"The doctrine of soul mates can be described as the belief that at some time a split occurred, separating the physical and spiritual natures of a person. The result of this split is that no human being can be complete within itself. The believers in the soul mate theory think it's necessary to be reunited with the other half of one's self in order to achieve perfection. This is a sad misunderstanding. Each person is complete within himself. Reincarnation and karma affirm the completeness of each person. Romantic infatuation is too often confused with the desire to find the other part of oneself, or one's soul mate."

All love relationships are reconnections from past lives. The intensity and the bond between these two souls is stronger because of the shared history. It's not unlike a friendship of twenty years compared to an acquaintanceship of just a few weeks. These relationships are not soul mated. They are karmic.

Sexual attraction is often misidentified as true love. This passion can be creative or destructive. There must be a firm foundation of mutual trust, respect, and friendship, as well as sexual attraction, in order to have a happy, balanced, committed love relationship. (I think that this is what people desire when they use the term soul mate.) But the fact is, there are many people on the planet at any given time with whom we could form a deep bond. Karma does play a part in the success or failure of our love affairs. It isn't always a past-life issue that causes our affairs of the heart to break up. We bring traits with us into this life that will affect the choices we make. These traits will also affect the way we react to situations. At the same time, our childhood has a lot to do with our current karma, in all our relationships.

Kathy Builds Her Future

One of my clients, Kathy, has been married four times. Each time she got married, she was certain she'd connected to her one true soul mate. After each breakup, she became extremely depressed. Kathy was kind and pretty; she was interested in art and loved literature and music. She'd spent most of her life getting in and out of marriages, so it was now time to involve herself in activities that were harmonious and also of a service to others.

I spoke to her for the first time right after her fourth marriage ended. I was able to point out some of her deep-rooted childhood traumas. Her father had died when she was three, and her stepfather had abandoned Kathy and her mother when Kathy was ten. Her mother, desperate to find another husband, constantly went out on dates, leaving her young daughter on her own. Kathy developed a deep fear of being alone. She believed that her happiness and security relied on having a man to marry.

Kathy's mother died never finding her "true love." Her dying words to her daughter were "You will never be happy unless you are married." Somewhere along the way, Kathy had picked up the idea of a soul mate, never quite understanding what it meant. What Kathy really was looking for was a way to stop the loneliness. Her mistake was believing that security and happiness could be found through external relationships. First, she needed to build a strong foundation *within* herself. Once she'd done this, Kathy would attract a man who was mature and in harmony with her. She needed to find the tools to help shape her low sense of self-esteem into a feeling of greater self-worth. "Maybe it's my karma to never find my one true love," she said sighing.

"Kathy," I replied, "you must not blame karma for your choices in husbands. It was karmic that you never had a good father figure and that your mother died. You can't change the past. Learn from it, and you will create new good karma. Work on ways to make yourself savvier in your ability to judge character. Take time to examine your own good qualities."

She'd acquired enough money from her last divorce to allow her some time without worrying about a job. Kathy admitted that sexual attraction was the basis for all her previous marriages. "Obviously, that alone isn't a firm enough foundation to build a life on," I said. Kathy laughed in agreement. She was also relieved that she'd not used up all her possible soul mates.

Kathy did finally attract a great man. But first she worked hard on her own inner strength. Kathy and her husband now have two children, and she is teaching her children to be independent, strong, loving, and kind.

LOVE, SEX, AND THE INTERNET

The phenomenon of the Internet affects not only our business lives but our personal lives as well. During the 1980s, and well into the 1990s, many clients came to me with questions concerning dating through the "personals." I can't tell you how many times people asked if they would meet a true love by answering a magazine ad. Yes, there are times this method has been effective, but that was because it was a person's karma to meet an appropriate person this way.

Today, searching cyberspace for love has joined personal ads, single bars, and dating services as a major vehicle for meeting possible lovers. Some people are using the Net as a dating service, others as a modern-day version of "phone sex," having sexual contact without meeting each other in person. I'm asked to psychically answer questions about Internet chat rooms almost daily.

Here are a few examples of what I'm hearing or being asked in reference to the Internet phenomenon: "What is the karma of cheating on your partner via computer?" "Will I find my true love searching cyberspace?" "Why is it so much easier to bare my soul to some one via E-mail?" "Should I hire a 'cybersleuth' to retrieve my husband's E-mails?" "My mother is addicted to chat rooms since my father died. Is this healthy?" "Do you think it's odd that my wife gets up in the middle of the night and goes online for hours at a time?" "I've never felt this way about anyone. I know we have never met in person, but the E-mails are amazing. Is this a past-life connection?"

Patty Learns That Typing Isn't Dating

Patty is twenty-four years old. She's terribly overweight and constantly anxious about it. A few years ago Patty began meeting men in Internet chat rooms. It was a way to try to establish relationships without having to meet face-to-face, as she was terrified of being rejected because of her size. Patty arrived to see me in a state of despair, and she related this story.

Patty corresponded with Mark on the Net for over a year before gathering enough courage to meet him in a public place. Their first encounter was in a coffee shop an hour from her home. "I knew the moment our eyes locked that I was in love. We talked for two straight hours, and he told me he loved me, too. Then he took my hand and asked me to go bed with him," she said.

They ended up going to a motel. She'd had only one sexual experience prior to this. Patty felt that she was giving herself out of love. Mark led her to believe that he loved her and accepted her as she was. He left telling her that he'd see her very soon. Patty was a bit upset with herself for hopping into bed with him so quickly, but she convinced herself it was destined.

She returned home and sent Mark an E-mail. He never responded, and a few days later he changed his E-mail address. Depression set in. Her visit to me was one of the few times she'd been able to leave her house. "He told me that he loved me," she kept repeating as she cried her heart out. Patty was reaping the karma for her behavior. She hadn't done her homework. She should have taken the time to discover Mark's true character.

"You're lucky that something worse didn't happen. He could have been a murderer, or a pervert, or given you a venereal disease. Typing is not dating," I told her. I predicted that she would find a nice guy. The Internet wasn't the problem. It was her lack of self-worth and lack of discernment. I told her to buy a *Power of Karma* Journal and instructed her on how to do the Exercise on Learning Discernment. She hasn't met Mr. Right yet, but she's becoming an expert in the art of discernment. I know that Patty will meet the right man, given time, and she knows it, too. By practicing the art of discernment, Patty is actively making good karma.

Mike's Mystery

Mike showed up in a tizzy. He felt his wife was having an Internet affair but couldn't prove it. I guess he thought I could play psychic Sherlock Holmes and solve the mystery. In this case it really was "elementary, my dear Watson." In fact, the clues were so obvious that Holmes wouldn't have taken the case. He would have forced Mike to face the music.

His wife was no longer having sexual relations with him. She stayed up until at least 4:00 A.M. sitting at the computer. They used to share a password, but his wife had changed that. When Mike asked her why, she snapped, "I just want to have my own." Mike said he felt guilty because he didn't have proof, but his wife's behavior made him feel something wasn't right.

"I see that your wife hasn't been intimate with you for over a year. Don't you think that's a long time, considering that you're still very attracted to her?" I waited for his reaction.

"It's not because I haven't tried," he said sadly.

"Mike, I don't think your wife is shopping on the Net every night until four A.M. What else can she be doing but using a chat room? I wish I could tell you that she was taking on-line college courses, but I don't see that. I think you'd be wise to confront this problem right away."

For a moment he was silent, and then he asked, "How do you feel about cheating via the Internet? Many people don't see this as infidelity because there is no physical contact with another person. I just don't know how to handle this. It's sort of crazy to feel jealous of a computer."

"What about fidelity of the mind and the spirit? To violate this involves serious karma, because the mental and spiritual links persist into future lives. The body dies, and the spirit lives on. The new technology is producing new karmic issues to ponder: Who would have thought that we'd have to deal with infidelity resulting from typing? Who would have thought an E-mail could be subpoenaed? We know that nothing dies, but who knew that nothing can ever be deleted? It's mind-blowing. But the Internet is here to stay." I paused.

"I wish it had never been invented," Mike said bitterly.

"It's people who choose how they use the Internet," I continued. "To blame it for your wife's infidelity is like blaming a wave for drowning a man who swam into uncharted waters." I paused again, then continued, "I think that your marriage has some real problems and that you had better get to the root of them by talking to your wife. This situation has gone on long enough. Go home and talk to her."

I didn't tell him that day that I saw a divorce in his future. He needed to face the problems, confront his wife, and try to work things out. I didn't want him to feel hopeless before he even attempted to reconcile their situation. The karma of their relationship should not be cut short, or it would be repeated in another life. Karma would provide a way to resolve their unhappy marriage.

I wondered if Mike was so naive in every aspect of his life. "Some things are just too painful to admit until they become intolerable. You just keep hoping that you're wrong, because the truth hurts too much," Mike said with tears in his eyes. "You must think I'm really stupid," he added.

"I think that you came to me so that I could confirm what you already know. That's not stupid—it's good sense. I do believe that you are too innocent about people's character, and this can cause you pain. Do try to learn and not repeat self-destructive patterns. You don't want to be one of the walking wounded," I said.

Mike returned to see me almost a year later. He had separated from his wife. They had gone to a therapist together, but his wife wouldn't stop her cybersex. She refused to admit that it was wrong. She believed that as long as there was no physical relationship, she wasn't cheating. Mike couldn't live with the pain of her betrayal, and after six months he left. Today he is still sad, but he's also relieved. "I couldn't fight with a computer for my wife's affection," he said with a smile.

"Mike, computers don't cheat, people cheat," I said as he left that day.

Take out three *pink* index cards and write:

1. Computers don't cheat. People cheat.
2. Typing is not dating.
3. Nobody dies, and nothing can be deleted.

You can't live without food or water, but you can live without sex. Sex can be beautiful, but we must keep the beauty alive by attracting relationships that are based on love. Think before you act. If you are attracted to someone who seems terrific—great! But take at *least* forty days (or forty times forty, if possible) before you begin a sexual relationship. Shouldn't you get to know a person before you allow a relationship to become physical? Is sex so important that you're willing to risk your life for it? We all need affection, but this can be received without having a sexual encounter. The God force lives within each of us. We are never alone. If we're busy serving and loving all whom we encounter in an unconditional way, we will not be preoccupied with thoughts of sex. We will have no trouble waiting for the right person with whom to express our love in a spiritual, sexual way.

Take out a *pink* index card and write:

You can't live without food and water, but you can live without sex.

5. Karma and Money

I believe that not one single client in the last twenty years has left an appointment without asking something about money. Everybody has some kind of money issue. These range from how to pay for education, health care, or credit card debt to requests for investment advice (I'm a psychic, not a broker!). Many people want to know if they will ever be rich. The rich ask if I see them remaining that way—or getting even wealthier.

Ever since Adam and Eve ate the apple and were booted out of Eden, the notion that "it's always money" became part of the world's karma. Their greed resulted in our need to make a living. In the beginning, the barter system was used rather than currency exchanges. For example, one could trade meat for fruit, wood for animal skins, or labor for food—a relatively simple system. Of course, today banks, insurance companies, Wall Street, and the like have made matters much more complicated.

Lawrence, who has an amazing knowledge of history, has

often talked to me about money. He tends to compare our modern life with that of ancient civilizations. He believes that there is much to learn by studying the way people used to live before most of humanity became consumed by the desire for transient material goods. That is, we live in an age in which "greed is good," in which we spend most of our time and energy procuring *things* that are not really necessary to our well-being. In fact, what satisfied the ancients would seem like squalor to us.

Commerce arose from the need for goods and services. Time passed, and people began to desire more things, more creature comforts. It was just plain practical to figure out a fiduciary system. So one of the greatest tests of our spiritual development became the way we handle money. Some people believe it's impossible to be spiritual in a material world. This is absurd. The world has always been materialistic to some extent. It's not the materialism that counts—it's the way we live within it.

On one hand, money can trigger jealousy, ulcers, heart problems, nervous breakdowns, divorces, unhealthy competition, corruption, lack of self-esteem, and despair. People with less money may despise those who have more. No wonder love of money has been called "the root of all evil"! However, it isn't right to suggest that we must be poor in order to live a good life.

On the other hand, money—the proper, balanced use of it—can bring you freedom.

Money can reduce stress when we have enough to pay our bills. It can provide us with comfortable homes, good food, nice clothing, education, health care, and recreation. Freedom from money worries can allow us more time to contemplate matters of the spirit. This freedom can provide us with a way to help others and to enjoy our family, friends, nature, and hobbies.

Money is freedom if a person has developed the wisdom to be detached from it. A secure person can live with or without it, and that is true freedom. Most people who pronounce that money is freedom are actually in bondage to making it, counting it, or worrying about not having it.

There's nothing wrong with having money. It's very simple, the law of karma says, "You get what you earn." If you have money, it's because you've earned the right to have it, in either this life or a prior one. A person concerned with living a life that is enhanced by good karma will accept wealth, live comfortably, and help others.

LOSE THE GUILT OR GAIN THE BOOMERANG

Emma has a huge trust fund left to her by her grandmother. She's spent ten years in therapy trying to learn how to deal with having a fortune. Relentlessly guilty, feeling she did nothing to earn this money, she wastes an enormous amount of energy being miserable.

She showed up to see me in a negative mood. I explained to her that she wouldn't have the money if she hadn't earned it in a past life. Didn't she ever wonder why she was born into a wealthy family? I stressed that their are no accidents in nature, and that we are born into our families because of karma.

"Emma, I'd lose the guilt if I were you. It shows a lack of gratitude, and it will cause you to reap bad karma. Why don't you spend your energy thinking of ways to help others with your money? Aren't you tired of being so silly?" I waited for her to reply.

"You mean I could be poor because I feel guilty. That doesn't seem fair," she curtly answered.

"Lots of poor folks would think it's unfair that such an ungrateful girl has been given so much. But you get what you earn, be it in this life or in a past one. Don't forget, Emma, every minute we are creating our current and future karma. That's why I'm suggesting that you stop the self-reproach. It's disgraceful. You could be having a great life, and all you do is complain. Of course, your behavior toward the money could cause you to be reborn into abject poverty. It could also cause you to lose the fortune in this life. And there are many things worse than being poor—cancer, blindness, lone-liness, to name a few. Think of all you have *besides* your money, and what it would be like to lose those things. I sug-gest you stop your negativity right now and start behaving with dignity, generosity, and gratitude. Find a charity you believe in, and donate some of your guilt money. There are thousands of ways to help through giving your finances. Don't just sit there feeling bad about your good fortune—do something with it, right away!"

I finished speaking. Emma sat very still for a few minutes and then simply said, "I will."

Emma had been given a lot to think about. I was surprised when she returned six months later a changed woman. She had stopped therapy and had started a scholarship for artists. It seems that the fear of poverty and her mortification were strong tonics for her guilt malady. She left our last session and was able to *just stop* feeling unworthy. Emma told me that my words about karma had hit her like a bolt of lightning. She was embarrassed by her previous lack of gratitude. I was happy for her and for the artists who would be served by her new point of view on inherited wealth.

Take out a *green* index card and write:

Gratitude is the first rule of spiritual development.

MONEY AND SELF-ESTEEM

The fallacy that money is a standard for character, and that lasting happiness will result from wealth and position, must be dispelled. There is no amount of money in the world that will give a person true self-esteem. This can be achieved only by living in harmony, in balance with all of nature. True peace of mind can't be bought. It can be earned by creating good karma in all areas of our lives. This, of course, has nothing to do with money.

Self-worth for many is based on relativity—if we have less than our neighbors, we can become miserable. The result is jealousy, and that can create the karma of a serious illness.

Take out a *green* index card and write:

True self-esteem can be obtained only through living in balance.

Louise Breaks an Obsession

Louise is a very attractive, successful businesswoman with a terrific husband and three wonderful sons. She has everything to be happy about, yet seemed very depressed when she walked in. Louise had recently been diagnosed with a non-malignant tumor in her mouth. As I observed her, I "saw" she'd had six benign tumors within the last six years.

Louise was jealous of her sister Martha's money. She was obsessed with her need to feel equal to her sister. Martha had married a multimillionaire and had two children. The family had a very elaborate lifestyle, and Louise was envious of that as well. I'd heard this story before. It sounded like material for a film noir script: sibling rivalry, delusions about money, envy, and a tragic end for at least one character. Louise was in physical, emotional, and spiritual trouble. She needed my help.

"Martha's always telling me about her new horses, trips, and all her rich and powerful friends. She doesn't include me in any of her plans. I'm treated like the poor pathetic relative. I tell her that I'm jealous of her lifestyle, and she says, 'Funny, I never feel envious of you.'"

"Louise, you're making yourself ill with your relentlessly morbid infatuation with Martha's financial status. Did you ever stop to think that it's your sister's karma to have what *she* has and it's your karma to have *your* life? You must find a way to stop your unbalanced behavior before you attract a more serious health problem. Why do you think you keep getting tumors? The energy isn't flowing out of your body in a healthy manner. Your deep lack of self-esteem, your rage over your sister's lifestyle, and your overall envy are causing these negative buildups. Stop this behavior, or one of these tumors might become malignant."

"What can I do? I just can't stand the fact that everybody knows she's the one with all the money. I introduced her to her husband, and she won't even credit me with that. What did I do in a past life that it's my karma to be so miserable?" Louise started to sob.

I felt pity for Louise. She was living in a dark tunnel of self-inflicted jealousy. Louise was convinced that a person's value was based on how much money they'd accumulated. She was clueless about karma. Her only hope for peace would come from changing her point of view. It would be tough to help her, but I was going to try.

"Louise, first get rid of the fantasy that your envy is a result of past-life karma. That's just a karmic cop-out. You are responsible for your attitude toward your sister in this life. Yes, there's a past-life relationship between the two of you. This isn't your first time together. Maybe you treated her with disrespect in a prior incarnation. But that's no excuse for your current behavior. Do you want to reincarnate and go through this test again?" I looked into her eyes as I waited for her reaction.

"You've got to be kidding! Do you mean I could go through this in another life?" she asked.

"No, I'm not kidding. And yes, you could. You have to balance any karma while you are on earth. If you don't get it right this time, you'll have to keep trying until you succeed."

"What about her karma?" she whined.

"I'm interested in yours for the moment, since you're the person here today."

"But, what am *I* doing to create such bad karma?" she asked.

"First, you are developing tumors because of your rage against Martha and her money. Second, you are creating negative karma because you lack gratitude for the great things you have in your own life. Third, you are wasting sacred energy on something that isn't a real problem. This will eventually cause you to attract one. Fourth, you are not being a good role model for your kids. Fifth, you can't change Martha; you can only change yourself. You're acting like a jerk. It's shameful," I said firmly.

At first Louise's eyes flashed indignantly, but she held her tongue as she pondered my words. "I never looked at it that way. All I saw was that people thought Martha was better because she's so much richer. I wanted Martha to give me credit for things, to make me feel important. Do you really think the tumors are brought on by my feelings of self-loathing? That's frightening. But you have to understand— all the people I know judge everybody by how much money they have." Louise paused and then started to cry again.

"I think you need to start spending time with some kinder people. Does your husband think like that?" I asked.

"No. He thinks that I'm crazy to keep trying to get Martha's approval. He doesn't care about money as much as I do. He feels that we have plenty and that I should enjoy our life. Now that I think about him, I realize that this obsession of mine must drive him crazy. He's a much nicer person than I am," she said through her tears.

"Louise," I said softly, "you must have some positive qualities, or he'd have left you by now. Don't negate the good things about yourself. Let's work toward finding ways for you to get over the negative and bring out the positive. You must release your obsession about your sister and rid yourself of the fixation that all people are valued by the amount of money they have. This is paramount in finding ways to shape your future into a healthier, happier, more balanced one. Your karma is in your hands!" I exclaimed.

"How do you break an obsession?" she asked.

BREAKING AN OBSESSION

"First and foremost, you need to understand what obsession is. Obsession has two meanings. Psychically speaking, it's a form of possession. You become possessed by your desire for something. This desire takes over your whole being and becomes a type of mental entity. The entity attaches itself to your mental body, to your aura, and it feeds itself from your repetition of an idea. To put it simply, you feed the entity by repeating, *Martha, money, Martha, money*, over and over, like a drumbeat. The entity becomes sympathetic to your negative mantra and keeps the obsession alive.

"The second meaning has a psychological basis—it is a fixation. The natural flow of the intellect is deviated because some idea has overcome the mind's ability to reason. Louise, you are obsessed by your desire to have your sister's money and her approval. This can be be remedied only through constructive thought. You must force yourself to replace the corrupt mantra of your compulsion with a sympathetic, harmonious one." I paused to see if she understood me.

"That's easier said than done," she said with self-pity.

I told Louise to take out a *green* index card and write:

Obsession can lead to insanity.

"It's easier to break an obsession than to get yourself out of a mental hospital. Keep up this relentless fixation and you'll become deathly ill or completely crazy," I said, shocking her.

"Is it really that serious? Is the entity the devil?" she asked with fear in her voice.

"Yes, it is very serious. No, it's not the devil. The devil wouldn't bother with such a silly little obsession. The negative force some people call the devil is much too busy trying to stir up wars and help inspire hatred, greed, or anything else that would negatively affect thousands of people. Why would it bother with a puny sibling rivalry? You and Martha aren't Cain and Abel, are you?" I joked.

"Tell me more about this entity stuff. I'm confused. It's scary," Louise added, at last hearing me.

"The type of entity I'm referring to is a nasty elemental. It is a life form that hasn't developed a physical body. Think of it as a spritelike being that hooks into your mind and loves to repeat nasty, useless ideas. It can continue only if you allow it to do so. Fear can be a good thing if it compels you to make changes in your life. You have reason to be frightened. You are courting disaster by your perverted thinking. Aren't you tired of living in your self-inflicted misery?"

We talked a bit longer and Louise agreed that she would make herself stop thinking about her sister's life and start thinking about her own. I told her to buy her index cards and a *Power of Karma* Journal.

Take out two *green* index cards and write:

1. An obsessive thought must be replaced with a constructive one.
2. A constructive thought is one that promotes health and peace of mind.

Examples of constructive thoughts are:

"All that is mine will come to me if I remain loving and kind."
"I am at one with the peace of good karma."
"I will focus on the good things in my life."

Use words like "friendship," "goodwill," "rapport," "at one," "useful," "healing," and "balance" in order to replace the obsessive words.

Your mind can't hold on to two thoughts at the same time. You will have to be vigilant and watch your thoughts like a hawk. The second you realize the negation fixation starting again, stop, breathe, and change the words *immediately*. Practice makes perfect, so do not give up. In time the obsession will have no power, and it will dissipate. Remember, you are the only one who can change your karma. Keep a record of your feelings in your *Power of Karma* Journal. This will help you to see the results of your labor.

As she left that day, I was certain Louise would win her battle. I'm happy to report that I was right. She returned a year later and hardly mentioned her sister. She was involved with her own work and family. She'd had no recurrence of the tumors.

Leo's Boomerang

Money has always been used as a measure of success or failure. People who are in the midst of financial hardship are often seen as lazy or pitiful. I've talked to people who are terrified to let anyone know they need work or financial assistance because they will be regarded as losers. That attitude is cruel and can boomerang upon the people who hold it.

Leo knows everybody. He's very prosperous and admired, and his success has given him ample leisure time. He once remarked, "The higher you go, the less you need to do, because you can pay people to do the legwork for you."

A good friend of Leo's lost his job and asked for help. Leo said, "Sure, I'll get right on it." His friend waited and finally called three weeks after the request. Not only had Leo done nothing to help, he hadn't even bothered to return his friend's call. It would have been so easy. A phone call of introduction would have made a great deal of difference to his out-of-work friend.

Time passed, and business turned south for Leo. He was voted out of his own company, and bad investments put him in the red. He started calling people to help him and was shocked when his calls were not returned. Boomerang!

Leo learned the hard way that "what goes around does

come around." "Do unto others as you'd like done unto yourself" became Leo's new favorite phrase. He is now very aware of the importance of helping others. I say, better late than never. Leo's still broke, but he seems a bit more optimistic that work is forthcoming, and by helping people, even in his newly limited way, he finally feels *good* about himself and his life.

I've observed many people who have made and lost fortunes. So be careful of being judgmental about other people's situations, financial or otherwise. Don't ignore a cry for help. The next cry you hear may be your own.

Here are a couple of good things to write on two *green* index cards:

1. Never ignore any opportunity to help someone.
2. The next person who needs assistance could be you.

Lawrence has said, "Money isn't so difficult to acquire. Almost anyone can achieve wealth if he is willing to sacrifice everything else to do so. It's a great deal easier to become rich than to be wise. Wealth isn't any measure of spirituality. The spiritual side is seen in the judgment used in doing good with one's riches."

FEAR

I find that many of my clients are plagued by feelings of fear. I have listened to panic in the voices of people terrified of being poor:

"My mother lived in constant fear that we'd lose everything. This never happened, but I live with the same fear."

"What will happen to me if I get old and have no money?"

"I am so sick, but I can't take the day off from work because I'll get fired and lose my benefits. I don't know where to turn."

"I know that I have millions, but I still worry about money. All my friends married rich guys. What if I can't find a rich one?"

When anyone is in a panic over money, I tell that person to write down the following questions in a *Power of Karma* Journal. Examine them and answer them with complete honesty.

1. Are you attracting bad karma by wasting sacred energy worrying about money when you have more than enough? Be careful. This could cause you to lose what you have, or you could be reincarnated with nothing.

2. If you don't have enough money to cover your needs, are you creating bad karma by focusing on the problem rather than finding a solution? Reverse the focus immediately. Remember, the first step toward changing your karma is changing your thinking. Negative thinking equals lack; positive thinking equals abundance.

3. Do you believe it's your destiny never to have enough money? Money karma, like any karma, can change in

the blink of an eye. If you don't have enough money today, this does not mean you will not have it tomorrow. You may have to work harder, change professions, or even move to a place with more opportunities. But you can earn more money.

4. Are you whining instead of working? Stop it!

FOR THE LOVE OF MONEY

Goethe said, "Everything in the world can be endured, except continual prosperity." As noted earlier, money in and of itself isn't the root of all evil. It's the selfish, do-anything-to-get-it, do-nothing-selfless-with-it, obsessive love of it that can be evil.

Judith's Plot

"I always get what I want!" These were the first words spoken to me by a woman named Judith.

"So why do you need to speak to me?" I asked.

"I thought it might confirm what I already know," she replied.

"Judith," I asked, "if you always get what you want, why are you angry that Harry doesn't seem interested in going to bed with you?"

"How do you know his name?" She looked almost frightened.

I explained that it was my gift as a psychic to know things about people without being told. "Judith, you are ruthless.

You'll take anything that isn't nailed down if you want it. That includes other people's husbands." I paused and looked for her reaction. She was unable to answer for a moment. I knew I was being tough on her, but I saw a lot of trouble for her down the road if she didn't examine her behavior.

"It's not my problem if a woman can't keep her man happy, and besides, I don't want him—I want what he can give me," she answered.

Just as quickly I asked, "How would you feel if someone went after *your* husband to get *his* money?"

"Let them try! And anyway, I don't have a husband. I couldn't be happy with just one man in my life. I need variety," she replied.

For a minute I thought she must be kidding. Few people are *that* ruthless. I studied Judith and knew she was dead serious. "So how do I get Harry?" She asked shamelessly.

"Be careful of what you ask for," I warned her. "I think you're heading into a storm, but you still have time to divert your course."

"Listen," she said, "I want a larger apartment and more money. Harry is the richest man I've ever met, and I want a piece of the pie. I'm certain if I can get him into the sack, he'll give me anything I want. I can tell Harry isn't happy with the sex he's getting at home, and I can remedy that problem. I don't love him, but I do like him well enough, and I *love* his money," she said with a laugh.

"Harry is married with three children. You should spend some time examining why you'd like to take on the bad karma for manipulating a man in order to get his money.

Don't you have any feelings for his family? You admitted that you don't even love him," I added.

"My success in life is linked to my success in getting men into my bedroom," she answered.

Judith's lack of knowledge about karma wouldn't protect her from the results of her actions. She just didn't care. She wanted the things that she felt Harry could give her, and that was that. I predicted she'd get him, but it would cause her a great deal of trouble. "You won't be happy, Judith. It's not too late to change your mind. I advise you to leave Harry alone and concentrate on finding a man who is free to be with you." I knew that she wouldn't take my advice.

Many months later Judith returned to see me. "You were right," she admitted. Judith had used her sexual expertise to lure Harry away from his family. He'd left home and rented an apartment for the two of them. Within months Harry went bankrupt. Judith had given up her own apartment and job when she moved in with Harry. She now had to start over with nothing. Harry's wife had filed for divorce, and Judith didn't want to be with Harry any longer. The stress caused Harry a mild heart attack, so Judith was letting him stay with her until he recovered.

"I finally understand what you meant by taking on karma for my actions. I'm paying the price for using Harry to get what I wanted. I realize that I was fooling myself with all my talk about not wanting a real love as well as money. Now I don't have either love or money," Judith told me. "How can I get rid of this bad karma?" she wanted to know.

"You can't *erase* bad karma. What's done is done. That's why we're encouraged to think before we speak or act. Life will present you with a situation in order for you to pay the price for your actions. You can learn a great deal from examining the past. It may help you not to repeat mistakes. For the present, Judith, you must be kind to Harry and help him get back on his feet. Think about Harry and not about yourself. Get a job, and promise yourself you'll never behave like that again. These actions will create new good karma for you," I told her.

Take out a *green* index card and write:

I can't erase bad karma, but I can learn and begin this moment to create good karma.

Judith's story isn't an uncommon one. Lots of people must experience the law of karma in action before it sinks in. Judith had used sex to get money. There was no love involved. She found out the hard way that if you intentionally hurt others with your actions, you will hurt yourself. Boomerang.

Pamela's New Rage

Pamela has an inheritance that allows her not to work. She is good-looking and has an excellent figure she can maintain without dieting. Her main form of exercise is walking the eleven blocks from Saks Fifth Avenue over to Bergdorf Goodman to shop, yet Pamela is a chronic complainer. She seems to have no trouble attracting men, probably because she is bright and has a witty side that some people find amusing. And her money doesn't hurt.

It seems she saw me as some sort of entertainment. But I think she found our session less than humorous. Pamela spent a great deal of her time with me fussing over her fingernails, quite distressed that she had broken one. She was like a character in a novel—the spoiled rich girl who looks at life as one long series of parties. Everything about her was chic: her clothes, her hairstyle, her address. She told me, though, that she was "bored, bored, bored!" While she didn't feel like traipsing off to Europe, she wanted to get away. She hated to go to the South of France out of season, and Italy had become too "common." She complained about New York's drabness and lack of charm, and no man she met was interesting enough to keep her entertained. She had been fed up at every party of the season, and just could not deal with the stupidity of her friends. I thought, *How can a person like this* have *any friends?*

I found myself fascinated by her, though. Certainly she aroused my curiosity. "What do you think I can do for you?" I asked.

"I want you to tell me about my future," she replied airily. "Isn't that what you're supposed to do? I want to be astonished by your ability to know things about me without my telling you anything," she said as she filed her nails.

"Pamela, this isn't a parlor game," I said. "I'm too busy to spend my time pulling rabbits out of a hat for your entertainment."

She seemed stunned but recovered her composure quickly. "Well, darling, I didn't mean to ruffle your feathers, but I needed something new and different, and I thought you could supply that for me."

I suggested that a better cure for her boredom would be for her to use some of her abundant wealth and time in trying to help others.

"Why should I do that? This is America. Can't people help themselves?" she asked.

Now it was my turn to be stunned. Her blindness to the suffering around her left me speechless as she went on to complain about everything and to wonder why people were so stupid and lacked "class." She perceived herself as more intelligent than anyone else. She thought her parents were stupid, her neighbors were low-class, and her friends were tiresome. I asked her if she ever read.

"No one is writing anything worth reading" was her reply.

"Pamela," I said as the session neared its end, "you must realize that this one life you are living is only a drop of water in the sea of eternity. If you don't wake up and try to do something for someone else, you'll have a very unhappy time in your next life. If you don't stop complaining and learn to have a bit of gratitude, you will be incarnated in your next life with *nothing, nada, zip*. How can you live with yourself? You do nothing but go on and on about how awful everything is and how boring all people are. If you would stop and take a good look at yourself and the emptiness of your life, you might have the good sense at least to be a little bit frightened. Wake up before it's too late! You have been *given* so much, and you actually think that the planet owes all this to you. You have no gratitude. I've never met anyone so self-involved."

I stopped, feeling that I might have gone a bit too far. I only hoped the shock treatment might wake her up a bit. But Pamela just batted her eyelashes and sighed, "Well, I had better be off. I want to get to Saks before closing. I need some night cream." She got up and said it had been marvelous to meet me. I could just as well have been talking to my refrigerator. I'd as much as told her that I saw her life as a worthless wasteland, and she'd shown no reaction at all! As she left, she complimented me on my "homey" apartment.

Feeling only relief, I closed the door behind her and started to laugh. You can't reach everyone. Ultimately, people have to decide for themselves how to live their lives. I could only do my best to point people in the right direction. Pamela must enjoy this state of negativity, or she would do something to change it. She might be shocked when she leaves the physical world and finds out that there is no Saks Fifth Avenue in the spirit world. Maybe something will happen to jar her awake, but it's a long shot. Her real problem is that she has too much money. Pamela is living proof that wealth isn't synonymous with happiness.

So I was completely surprised ten months later when Pamela called to make another appointment with me. "Why do you want to see me again, Pamela?" I asked. "I don't think there's anything I can do for you."

"Oh, I just felt it was time for a checkup," she replied.

"Pamela," I said, "I'm not your dentist."

As usual, she was unfazed and just pressed on. "Well, I

have thought about the things you told me, and I think your idea of trying to be grateful is rather interesting. I don't really understand it, but I thought we might chat about it again if you could find some time for me."

I hesitated for a moment, wondering whether there would be any point to another session, but I gave her an appointment.

She arrived at the scheduled time, loaded with shopping bags and out of breath. "I hope I'm not late," she said. "I was having lunch with my girlfriend, and she was so newsy that the time just sped by."

"Did you have a nice lunch?" I asked.

"The food was positively dreadful," she replied. "And the atmosphere! I thought I had lost my way and ended up in a greasy spoon. You just cannot get good service anymore." She paused to take a breath. "You look great, Mary T. Where did you find that little dress?" she asked.

"I don't remember, dear," I answered. I thought that this would be a very long hour as Pamela chatted on and on, not giving me much of an opportunity to say anything. Finally I managed to interject, "You said on the phone that you wanted to hear more on the subject of gratitude."

"Yes, I do. I've never heard anyone speak about it in the way you did. Is it part of a new type of psychology?" she asked.

Trying to conceal my astonishment, I said, "Haven't you ever been thankful for anything?"

"Of course." She laughed. "Thanking people is a sign of proper breeding."

"That's not exactly what I meant," I said. "Have you ever

felt grateful for all the good things you've been given in your life?" I waited for her reply.

She looked at me blankly, as though this were an alien concept. I'd actually managed to say something to which she had no reply. I used the opportunity to tell her that all the advantages she enjoyed and took for granted—her appearance, her health, her material possessions, her family and friends—were really great gifts, and that she should be deeply thankful for all these things and more. I could see that she still didn't understand, so I suggested she make a list of everything positive in her life, all the things she could be grateful for. I told her to buy a special journal and label it *Power of Karma*.

Her face lit up, and I thought for a moment I'd made a connection, that at last she understood. But then she began to babble excitedly about what a wonderful idea this was for a new party game: a kind of scavenger hunt in which everyone would be required to compile a list of things to be grateful for. The person who came up with the longest list in the shortest time would be the winner. She would buy all her friends a journal, because she knew where the best ones were sold. I started to object, but then I thought, *Who knows? Maybe one guest at the party will learn something from this.* If so, it would be worthwhile.

As Pamela was leaving, she thanked me for coming up with an idea that she thought would become the "new rage." *Wouldn't it be wonderful,* I thought, *if that were so—if gratitude became the "new rage"?* Certainly it would help to make the planet a happier place. Pamela's motivation wasn't selfless, but nothing ventured, nothing gained.

DON'T STEAL FROM THE UNIVERSE

There is an outrageous, dangerous belief among certain metaphysical, mind-control, or so-called spiritual movements. These groups contend that the universe itself is interested in the finances of its devotees. The "proof" of true "illumination" is the constant flow of money into one's hands without lifting them in honest work. "Prosperity consciousness" is a term used for attracting money in this manner.

You may wonder what I mean by "in this manner." Visualization, concentration, incantation, meditation, and contemplation are practices that demand that you control your thoughts in order to attain something. These practices by themselves are neither negative or positive. It is the motivation of the person invoking them that decides whether good or bad karma is attracted into one's life. If the desired result is materialistic (money, power, sex) instead of spiritual (security, love, harmony, selflessness), negative karma will result.

You can work with a positive attitude, and with even a small amount of cleverness you can honestly acquire more money. There's no negative karma because you got what you earned. But you must beware: Taking money or anything else that you haven't earned through your own positive labors creates bad karma. This is very dangerous—physically, mentally, spiritually, and, of course, karmically.

Carol and that Old Black Magic

Carol believed that the universe owed her money. She came to see me demanding to know when I saw money coming to her. Lured by promises of riches, she practiced many manifestation techniques and then waited for her wishes to come true. She became so bewitched with her desire to attract all the money the universe "owed" her that she spent every dollar she made on workshops, tapes, lectures, psychic readings, and the like. Eventually she was fired because she missed so much work choosing to attend seminars rather than showing up for her job.

Her condition distressed me. She had the glazed look that I'd seen in the eyes of people who were members of a cult. Kindly, I tried to explain the law of karma to her. She continually interrupted me, asking about money...money...money—until I was forced to tell her to shut up. My abrupt words shocked her into silence. I used this method because I feared she was heading for disaster, and I was desperate to help avert it, if possible.

"Any use of occult powers in order to manifest our personal desires is a misuse of the force and can be called black magic," I declared. She looked at me as if I were speaking a foreign language. So I gave her this detailed explanation: "We are protected only by our own goodness. If you hold on to a thought and isolate it from others, you call into existence a form. Each form becomes an elemental. An elemental is an invisible entity at a primitive stage in its evolution.

These entities are also known as fairies, sprites, elves, brownies, pixies, leprechauns, trolls, goblins, banshees, and so on. They can become visible if you are clairvoyant. But don't fool yourself. Just because *you* can't see them doesn't mean they are not there. A blind man has never seen color, but he knows it exists. An elemental acts upon instructions from humans. These directions come from powerful thought forms created by repetition and mind control. They act in accordance with how they are instructed.

"Just think: If you get money, it has to come from someone. Let's say that you decide you're going to find a hundred dollars. You sit in deep concentration and repeat, over and over, 'I will find one hundred dollars.' You then perform a mind-control exercise in which you see yourself walking down the street finding that exact sum of money. The power of these thoughts attracts an elemental to do the work for you. It may take you weeks or months to see the result of your selfish action. But one day you will be walking down the street, look down, and find the money. Don't get too excited. Somebody had to lose his money in order for you to find it. This could have been a person's welfare check, your grandma's Social Security benefit, a student's book allowance, or somebody else's mad money. Bottom line: It wasn't, and isn't, your money." I paused and then continued, "The elemental was able to distract the victim by giving the person a thought form that caused him or her to drop the money. For example, Grandma, having just cashed her Social Security check, ready to put the money in her purse, starts to worry that she left the iron on. The distraction causes her to drop the money on the street while thinking she put it into her purse. The elemental put the idea of the iron into Grandma's mind. This is what is meant by stealing from the universe. Your intense thought form caused another human being to lose her money, so you could find it. I promise you that sooner or later, at the worst possible moment, you'll find your wallet empty. Boomerang! You lost your money, or your pocket was picked," I finished the explanation and waited for Carol to respond.

She merely stared at me and said nothing. So I added, "Look at your own life. You've lost everything trying to get *more* with *less* effort. Can't you see the boomerang? Positive thinking combined with the appropriate action will bring you good things. Why play with forces you don't understand?" I asked.

Carol finally spoke. "Mary T., when, exactly, do you see me finding the money?" Carol has not returned to see me.

Take out a *green* index card and write:

Positive thinking combined with appropriate action brings good karma.

KARMA AND BANKRUPTCY

You must pay your debts. By now I've repeated this fact over and over again. With this in mind, a serious question arises. When is declaring financial bankruptcy a karmically acceptable decision? This is a difficult spiritual issue. If you've done everything humanly possible to avoid bankruptcy, only then should you consider filing for it. What do I mean by "everything"?

Take out your *Power of Karma* Journal and answer the following karmic questionnaire. Copy these questions and record your answers next to them. Your responses will help you honestly evaluate your financial situation.

1. Have you taken a second or third job in order to pay off debts?
2. Have you spent one unnecessary dollar instead of paying a bill?
3. Have you contacted everybody to whom you owe money and tried to work out a payment schedule?
4. Have you changed your lifestyle to reduce your monthly outlay of money?
5. Have you cut up your credit cards?
6. Have you sold everything of value in order to raise funds?
7. Have you sought professional advice from every available avenue—magazines, books, television, wise friends?

I have had many clients over the years who did all these things and were still unable to satisfy their creditors. The circumstances that caused the financial devastation were out of their control. For some, the economy changed quickly, and businesses that were booming boomeranged. For others, a responsible risk on a legitimate business deal went bust. And most tragically, in some instances an illness in the family emptied bank accounts and took property, leaving no alternative but to borrow cash advances from credit cards at exorbitant interest rates. In cases such as these, bankruptcy is an acceptable spiritual decision.

Herbert Bites the Bullet

My client Herbert found himself in one of these terrible situations. Herbert was very depressed when he came to see me. He had used all his savings and had taken a second mortgage on his house in order to start his own business. Working eighteen hours a day, he was losing weight and was anxious all the time. No matter how hard he tried, the bills kept piling up, because there just wasn't enough business. Then the area Herbert lived in went into a recession without warning. Herbert sold his good car, put his kids in public schools, tried to sell his house, and still couldn't make it. His wife, Lucy, sold home-baked cakes and cookies in order to help out. She had tried to find a job—but there were none available. Herbert was on the verge of a nervous breakdown.

I told him that I did not see his bleak business outlook changing anytime in the near future. We discussed options, and all I could see was bankruptcy. I saw in his aura that he'd suffer a total collapse, or even death, if he didn't lighten his load. Kindly, but firmly, I told Herbert what I saw.

Herbert did not take my message lightly. He put his head in his hands and began to cry, more out of fatigue than self-pity. He closed his business and filed for bankruptcy soon after our session. The family moved into a small apartment, and he found work in a friend's hardware store. Lucy is still selling baked goods, and the kids are doing fine in public school. Herbert is humiliated that he was unable to pay his debts. But he finds comfort in knowing that he did everything humanly possible in order to balance his karmic bank account. Only when every avenue was exhausted did he bite the bullet. Herbert is a clear example to all of us of a karmically acceptable, spiritually balanced decision for filing bankruptcy.

Kelly's Caught in the Act

Kelly arrived wearing expensive designer clothes. "All new," she bragged as she sat down. She was about twenty-five, tall, slim, with a haircut reminiscent of a Jazz Age flapper's. She looked at me and said, "I've just declared bankruptcy, so I can afford to see you today."

"I hope you're joking," I replied.

"No," she said.

"I ran up my credit card bills to thirty thousand dollars. I could hardly meet the interest payments, much less pay off any of the principal. So I decided to go bankrupt."

"This doesn't bother you at all?" I asked.

"Why should it? Everybody does it" was her reply.

"No, Kelly, everybody does not declare bankruptcy, and your attitude is going to get you into deep karmic trouble. You haven't cleared your debt; you only think you have. You didn't attempt to put your affairs in order. You spent money on things you didn't need and then just decided to tell everybody to go jump in the lake. One way or another, life will force you to grow up and accept responsibility for your actions. Now you're boasting that you can afford to see me because you took advantage of others. What planet did you grow up on?" I asked.

"How do you know I bought things I didn't need?" she challenged me.

"I'm sorry, Kelly, I guess everybody does need fourteen pairs of Manolo Blahnik shoes."

"That's the exact number of pairs I have." She was visibly startled by this psychic tidbit.

Yet Kelly had no remorse. She acted as if the world owed her whatever she desired. She boasted that she had already gotten a new credit card through a friend's connection. She couldn't wait to go shopping—again.

I stressed that in one way or another she'd have to pay the piper. She was living off other people's money. I also added that I saw income tax problems for her in the not-too-distant future. At this point she admitted she'd worked some free-lance jobs but never filed her taxes. Nonetheless, Kelly left our session acting as though everything were just fine. She'd not heard a word I'd said.

A year and a half later I ran into a friend of Kelly's. Kelly had been caught by the IRS. Unable to come up with the back taxes she owed, she'd been forced to leave New York and move back in with her parents in Albany. They were not sympathetic to her lack of respect for money. She's now working double shifts as a waitress to pay the taxes and giving her parents whatever she has left over. She sold her shoes at a thrift store for almost nothing. Boomerang!

Take out four *green* index cards and write:

1. I will do everything humanly possible to pay all my debts before I even consider bankruptcy.
2. If I abuse money in this life, I will be born with none in the next one.
3. There can be no erasures in the universal karma bank.
4. Debts have no deadline.

I wonder if people consider that they will reincarnate with nothing but money problems if they abuse money in this life. Why do you think certain people are born into poverty instead of comfort? Certainly a major factor in having bad money karma comes from behavior in prior lives. Kelly's case could have past-life roots, but clearly her behavior in this life was enough to create bad karma. She'll keep coming back to earth and messing up if she doesn't learn an important lesson: The proper handling of money is one of the greatest tests the spirit is given. Don't blow it!

KARMA AND CONTRIBUTION

We are living in a world where one-quarter of humanity is in a position to affect immediate relief on the suffering of the rest of the planet. Each person has the opportunity to contribute as much money or labor as he or she can in order to alleviate the suffering of others. Many who enjoy the gift of money have no conflict with charity. These individuals have an innate desire to help others. They never give to get something back. They give because it is as natural as breathing—the right thing to do. It's part of being an integrated person in the world.

We can create very bad karma through our lack of awareness of the needs of those less fortunate than ourselves. People come to me and say, "When I'm rich, I will start a charity." I've never heard anything so narcissistic in my life. What—you want a hospital wing with your name on it? A chair at a university? A stained glass window in a cathedral? My response is "What are you waiting for! Start today. How about a buck for the homeless?"

Take out your *Power of Karma* Journal and write down these simple suggestions for shaping your contribution karma.

1. Take time to look around. See how you can contribute at this very moment.
2. Do any action you can to help others. It doesn't need to be a grand gesture. A dollar from a person who has little is just as valuable as a million dollars from a very wealthy person.
3. Dollars alone don't constitute generosity. Your time can be donated to a cause if you don't feel you have any extra money.
4. You can learn to be a giver if it's not innate to you. The beauty of desiring to be of service will help to affect the balance of the world karma as well as your own!

Don't you want to help others because it's a great thing to do? Every day I walk by the Village Nursing Home in my

New York City neighborhood. I've gotten to know many of the folks who live there. On nice days the tenants sit outside in their wheelchairs and enjoy watching people go by. A few words to these lovely people can make their day. It's so easy to say, "Hello, how are you?" It's easy to help rearrange their chairs if they want to sit in a sunnier spot. One of my special friends is a man named Harold, who likes to show me the latest pictures of his beloved baby granddaughter. It's a joy to watch him laugh and smile as he shares the pictures. It takes maybe five minutes to help a person feel important. Many people in Greenwich Village are aware of the folks at the nursing home. And, sadly, many are not.

All you have to do is look around you as you walk, and you'll find a way to create the beautiful karma of contribution. This isn't just money! It's kindness, cheerfulness, interest in someone else. We will all be old one day if it's our karma to live a long life. Don't you hope somebody will notice if *you* are sitting in your wheelchair looking for a few words of encouragement? This action doesn't require any money or much time. All it takes is a little energy. Love begets love, in case you forgot.

It's so much easier to be kind than to be neglectful. It's so much easier to be aware than to live in the darkness of denial. I've never met a happy selfish person. We were born to contribute, which is a fact some of us have forgotten. I don't want to hear any excuses, such as "I can't help myself, so how can I help someone else?" The simple act of reaching out to another human being could break your negative karma pattern and start the flow of good things toward yourself.

People may be motivated to give because they believe this will guarantee that their "gift" will be returned in some way. This is not a positive action, because the reason for giving is selfish. Many very rich people donate enormous amounts of money with grand gestures and press conferences. Often this is a way to avoid income tax *and* get some good press as well. Yes, the money can help people in need. But this isn't true generosity, because it's an ego trip for the donor. The real joy of contribution is in the act of doing it regardless of recognition. But recognition or not, give of yourself, whenever you can. Enjoy the act of giving. Honor it. Remember that we are all karmically connected.

Take out a *green* index card and write:

The homeless person you neglect could be you in another life.

The next time you see a homeless person on the street, take a *real* look at her. That could be you in another life if you ignore her. Some people say we must teach others to become self-sufficient, and that means no "handouts." Great. It's practical to show someone how to plant the seeds that will produce food from one year to the next. But until people have the seeds, the land, the tools, and the knowledge, we may have to give them food and water.

Take out your *Power of Karma* Journal and practice this exercise in awareness:

Write down at least one action of goodwill that you do each day. It could be giving a dollar to a homeless person, saying a kind word to someone at work, spending an hour reading to the blind, or doing whatever else comes your way.

This will help you see the harmony that comes from the good karma of any contribution given to anyone from your heart. Keep it simple, but be consistent.

The Wedding

Last fall I received a message from Lawrence to meet him in Santa Fe, New Mexico. This wasn't a great surprise, because I often go there to visit two lovely ladies whom I look after. We'd be able to catch up and take care of business at the same time. When I arrived at my hotel, the phone was ringing. "My child, I see you are here on time," Lawrence said. He told me to rest, as I'd had a long trip to New Mexico from New York. He said he'd meet me at one of my favorite spots at four o'clock the next afternoon.

It was a perfect day. I drove to a little town called Ojo Caliente, about an hour outside Santa Fe. The town gets its name from its famous mineral springs. Lawrence and I met at a funky little café in the middle of town.

Lawrence has the uncanny ability always to look at home no matter where we meet. He arrived wearing a blue denim shirt, khaki pants, and loafers. A blue jacket was draped casually over his arm. He was smiling with a twinkle in his eyes. "Adaptability is an art," he said as he took my hand.

I laughed. "With you, Lawrence, it's a science."

We ordered lunch and sat quietly for a few minutes. Lawrence knew what had been going on in my life. As I mentioned earlier, he is able to read my thought forms and is only a thought away when I need him. He wanted to check on my progress with this karma project and to answer some questions I'd been pondering. He broke the silence by saying, "Tell me about the wedding you attended last month."

A very wealthy socialite client of mine had had a grand wedding for her only daughter. It was a spectacular affair and received a lot of attention in the press. The guest list was a social "who's who," and the affair was held at the best hotel in New York. There was no expense spared in order to pull off the wedding of the year. I'd attended because I like this client a lot and had known her for ten years. It was a great party, and everybody was having fun.

"Well, it was amazing," I answered. I told Lawrence the details and added that I wanted to know his opinion of spending two million dollars on a wedding.

"Think about how many people your friend employed. The dressmakers, the florists, the hotel staff, taxi drivers, waiters, food and wine suppliers, shoemakers, department store clerks, and on and on. This was a help to the city's economy, everyone had a nice time, and your friend had no trouble affording it. The lady who threw the wedding for her daughter is a very philanthropic person," he answered.

I must say his reply surprised me. Lawrence had read my thoughts. "Why are you so amazed at my answer? You are trying to teach people about practical ways to create good karma and to help others, are you not? I believe the wedding served dual purposes. Everyone had a wonderful time so their joy sent positive thought forms throughout the city, and people were helped by making money," he added.

"Of course, you're right. I hadn't thought about it in quite that way. The money for the wedding did help a lot of people, and, after all, it's her money to use as she chooses. There would be no economy if people didn't spend money on goods and services," I replied.

"Exactly," he agreed, pleased that I got it.

"People expect teachers to shake their fists at such excess," I added.

"That wouldn't be very adaptable of me." He paused as our lunch arrived. "The world economy is served by such goings-on. We can't change the fact, so we must see the merits and not the flaws of such spending."

Lawrence is the most flexible person I've ever met. He has helped me a lot over the years to be less rigid and more adaptable in all areas of life. You'd think it would have been the other way around, that a man of his great spiritual development would have more definite stands on issues. He is very certain about his feelings, but he possesses the quality of understanding the way in which others perceive situations.

ADAPTABILITY

Lawrence spoke about the need for humankind to become more adaptable. "Change must come from within. Most people believe that if they change their hair or their wardrobe, they will be changed. Not true. Only when one works on the inner self does one feel the effects of change."

"How can I help people become more open to change?" I asked him. "I think many people would suffer less if they prepared more. For example, look at the economy. People are freaking out because the stock market has been fluctuating so wildly. There's a lot of fear and anger. People see their portfolios going down, and they don't have the excess income they've become used to. It seems that a great number of people put all their eggs in one basket. They put their money in technology because the returns were enormous. Then one day it all started to boomerang. The downturn should have been anticipated, because it's absurd to think that anything can keep growing at such a fast rate forever. Many of my clients are depressed and panicked about their financial futures. I don't want to see everyone living in total paranoia. But to deny that the world is changing before our eyes is foolish." I waited for his reply.

He nodded in agreement. "It never hurts to remember that history indeed repeats itself. Financial markets have always gone up and down. They will continue to do so. What does it serve to become hysterical about things that you can't control? People react violently when they feel they are not ready for change. It is rare that life waits until we feel totally ready, but if you start to prepare before a crisis, you will not be thrown out of balance when the change occurs. Education is necessary in order to be able to adapt. People do not know how to have a better life. They become locked in the familiar, and anything out of the ordinary seems intimidating," Lawrence paused.

"That's the rub, people can't or won't change, until they are given no other choice," I added.

"Adaptability depends on having a strong sense that the circumstances of life are presented for our growth. If a person attracts a situation, karmically speaking, it is because he needs to learn something. No matter how bad the problem seems, it will pass. Time is a great healer as well as an intelligent teacher. More than anything else, it takes time to integrate change. And a sense of humor never hurts." He paused again and took a sip of tea. "It appears I must adapt to the lateness of the hour."

He took my hand, walked me to my car, and suggested I spend some time contemplating what we had discussed. I marveled at the beauty of the sunset over the mountains. I felt deep gratitude to be able to enjoy nature as I focused on adaptability and how all "real change" comes from within.

This simple exercise will help you if you are overwhelmed by financial worries. Take out your *Power of Karma* Journal.

1. Ask yourself, "How many hours a day do I spend thinking about money, and how many do I spend thinking about my spiritual development?" Write down the answer. Ask yourself this question, and record your answers, for the next seven days.

If at the end of a week you realize that your finances dominate your thinking, consume most of your time and energy, and leave you exhausted, it's time to adapt your focus. Obviously you are not spending enough time on things of the spirit. You may be wondering how this adaptation is achieved.

2. Adjust your thinking. Simply raise your consciousness to think about things that will promote balance. A few

examples are friendship, love, nature, music, and, most important, serving others.

3. Take a few minutes as many times during the day as you can to focus the mind on elements of spiritual beauty.

4. At the end of each day jot down a few words to let yourself know how you're feeling.

You will be amazed to find that worry has been replaced by greater harmony. These treasures are not physical but spiritual. They can't be affected by the fluctuations in the financial markets. They are available to everyone at all times. Once this adjustment has taken place, you will feel a significant change in your disposition. Worry will have been replaced by greater peace of mind.

6. Karma and Power

Power is fleeting. Political, economic, and social conditions can change in a flash. Newspapers are full of accounts of coups d'états, corporate takeovers, political scandals, and economic turmoil. These events lead to drastic changes in leadership in many arenas. One minute someone is the "boss," the next an underling. Power struggles can destroy our families, our friendships, and our romantic relationships.

People are drawn to those in power. Often people believe they become more influential if they are seen in the company of the powerful. What we have to remember is, power isn't only the birthright of sovereigns, the reward of military promotions, or the result of political victories. It doesn't live only in the corner offices of Fortune 500 CEOs. There are many types of power, be it financial, political, social, emotional, or spiritual.

Let's face it, we all desire to have some amount of power in our lives. We all need to feel some sense of importance, authority, significance, and value in our worlds. For many, this recognition lies in their influence at home, at work, at church, or in community affairs.

Power can, and should, have a positive influence in our lives. Its proper use can make our lives much more harmonious and balanced. Have you ever experienced the wonderful feeling that comes from having the strength to resist a temptation, such as smoking, overeating, or succumbing to irrational bursts of temper? Have you taken time to help someone who feels left out and alone? This action of sharing your power with someone weaker strengthens both of you. Good bosses use their authority in a way that makes workers feel respected and needed. But certain types of power can disappear in the blink of an eye. So let's fight to establish *real* power. That which is real lasts. It's not dependent upon externals.

Lawrence spoke to me about authentic power. "Genuine power is reflected in the internal qualities of a person. These qualities are earned by the positive use of the will and the constant striving to create good karma through thinking and acting in a manner that benefits humanity. People who only want power, and live for it, neglect everything else in their lives. Family, love, and health are a few of the ignored aspects that fall aside to make a clear path for power. When the power drive is too extreme, people lose their link to other human beings. Sooner or later some type of failure enters their world, causing loneliness, physical or mental depletion, or even premature death."

Take out two *purple* index cards and write:

1. Power should have a positive position in my life.
2. Genuine power is reflected in my internal qualities.

Leonard's Power Failure

Nothing could stop Leonard from working too hard. He spent long hours at his office and gave himself little or no "downtime." As a result he suffered a slight stroke. He was hospitalized and firmly warned by his doctor that he must slow down. Leonard's wife was very worried, but he wouldn't listen to her. She tried to persuade Leonard to lighten up, but he snapped at her to stop nagging him. He left the hospital and a day later went right back to work. He wouldn't delegate; he felt that he was the only one who could do his job properly. Leonard fell into his same old routine: working late, poor diet, no exercise. He kept repeating that he wanted to be a multimillionaire by the age of forty. His wife didn't care about great wealth. They were very comfortable, and she thought Leonard should be grateful for what they had and try to enjoy life more. But he wouldn't take a day off—no matter what. He felt that time was money, and money was power. Leonard came to see me once. I warned him that I saw he wouldn't live to forty if he didn't slow down. He just kept asking if I saw him moving into a position of greater wealth and power.

At the age of thirty-nine Leonard dropped dead from a heart attack. This tragedy was so unnecessary. If Leonard had heeded the warnings of his doctor, his wife, and me, he would probably be alive today. When I spoke to his wife after the funeral, she said she wished she'd been firmer with her husband. I assured her that she had done all she could to help him. This was the tragic case of a man who died too young because of his ambition.

"Ambition can be a terrible thing," Leonard's wife said through tears of grief. "It's ridiculous when you think about it. Leonard had everything to live for, but it never seemed to be enough."

"Power can corrupt. He couldn't see the forest for the trees," I told her gently. "Workaholism" is chic nowadays, but it gains you nothing if you end up a statistic. You can do a very good job and make a fine living without killing yourself. I know a man named Henry who heads a huge corporation yet never seems overloaded with concerns about work. If his week has been particularly trying, he leaves the office early on Friday. Never neglecting a thing, he refuses to kill himself because of the job. He took a great deal of time choosing an excellent staff, and he knows that a good boss is a person who can delegate responsibility. He recharges by going to the country as often as possible. "Temperate" is a word I would use to describe him.

He told me, "I don't drink to excess, nor do I eat or exercise to excess. I live every day with a sense of moderation."

It isn't necessary to be a corporate head to acquire genuine power. It's possible for everyone to live life as this man does. It may seem difficult at first, but it's easier than living with constant anxiety. Henry has *real* power. He is in control of his life, it doesn't control him.

Avoiding Power Failures

We all have times when we feel overloaded by work or life in general. For every task we complete, it seems that two more spring up in its place. But we force ourselves to soldier on— even when our energy is short-circuited.

Here are a few simple exercises for avoiding power failures.

1. Don't live each day as if on deadline. This will shorten your life and make you ill tempered. Listen to your body; it will tell you in no uncertain terms if it is overloaded. Stress manifests itself through a wide range of physical symptoms, including digestive disorders, sleeplessness, nervous tremors, skin rashes, and heart problems. Pay attention to warning signs and slow down. If you do take heed, you will save yourself from more serious problems.

2. Prepare for stressful times by relaxing when you can. This will give you the added "juice" you need to meet a particular deadline.

3. Take a moment and ask yourself, "What's the use of driving myself to the breaking point?" You are not judged by your bank account or your title when you pass over to the other side, but only by how well you have served others. Service is the true measure of the quality of life.

4. Ask yourself at the end of each day, "What did I do today to serve another?"

Simple adjustments in our behavior can protect us from depleting our power reserves. Here is an exercise that is practical and potent:

Take five minutes every morning to mentally organize your day. I realize that most of us are very busy, but this can be done while making coffee, shaving, taking a shower, or packing your child's lunch. Use this time to focus on the *needs* of this particular day. Remember the word "need": it means the *essential* duties of this particular twenty-four-hour period. Do not confuse what you *need* to do with what you want to do or wish you had time to do.

Your mental "essentials" list may go something like this:

Have breakfast. Get to work on time. Attend a business lunch at noon. Concentrate on the clients who must be handled today. Arrange to have dry cleaning delivered. Confirm dinner reservations with girlfriend. Do fifteen minutes of stretching exercises before bed. Set the alarm for tomorrow.

Another list may be:

Make certain everybody is awake. Make coffee; remind husband to pick up flowers for his mother's birthday on the way home from work. Offer everybody some breakfast. Walk the kids to the school bus. Straighten the house. Pay the monthly bills. Run errands—grocery shop, post office, school supplies. Take a nap. Pick up the kids from the bus stop. Spend time with them. See Grandma for her birthday.

Now, it probably took less then five minutes to prepare that mental appointment book. Don't allow yourself to panic over the things you don't have time to fit into your day. Such upset will only serve to deplete much-needed energy. Do this exercise every morning for at least forty days. Observe the change in your outlook. You should find yourself more centered, happier, and more balanced. I believe that when you realize how helpful this exercise is, you will continue after the forty days—maybe even for the rest of your life.

AMBITION

Ambition is always negative. When we desire to do our very best, whatever the circumstance, we are spiritually motivated. There's a big difference between ambition and spiritual motivation. Take, for example, the difference between assertion and aggression—it's the difference between a handshake and a slap in the face.

Ambition is the desire for worldly success or power. It's colored with envy and conjures up images of exploitation, aggression, and greed. The driving force of ambition is advancement of status. Ambition is the antithesis of humility and spiritual balance. An ambitious person is self-absorbed and most often quite obnoxious. It's a misunderstanding of the word's meaning to believe that ambition is a positive attribute. It can be an element in the makeup of a power seeker, but the result is most often a power failure.

Lawrence spoke with me about ambition. "You will hear people say that if they were not ambitious, they would have accomplished nothing in their lives. This is not the case. Remember, the law of karma teaches that we get what we earn. Should our attitude be one of stress and struggle or calm and resolution? You can work hard and focus your energies on doing a good job without being enslaved by ambition. Ambition can hurt others. A person can become so involved with his personal pursuit for power that he ignores everyone else. Is it worth hurting or even destroying others in order to get what you desire? You can be a caring, responsible person and still have success with your work."

Take out two *purple* index cards and write:

1. I will not be a slave to ambition.
2. I will focus my energy on excellence, not on pursuing power.

Merrill's Methods Miss the Mark

Merrill was obsessed with ambition. Determined to climb the corporate ladder, she was relentless in her pursuit of a higher title. She worked sixteen hours a day and had no life outside her job. She slept fitfully, was always worried that she had not done enough work, and was testy and ill natured. In truth, no one liked her. Like a robot, she would work regardless of how she felt. She was sick for three months one winter but never took a day away from the office to rest. She lost touch with friends because she was too busy working to return phone calls. Finally people stopped calling.

I asked her about this, and her answer was that she was going to get the promotion no matter the price. Her father had once told her she would never amount to anything, and she was going to prove him wrong even if it killed her. Her face was fixed in a scowl of total, unwavering determination. Merrill listened to no one, certainly not to me. I warned her that if she did not slow up, she would suffer a nervous breakdown. She had come to me to find out when her promotion would come through. "Merrill, I honestly don't see a promotion. You have some competition at the job that you're unaware of, and I see you in your current position for at least another year," I predicted. She stormed out.

Time passed, and when the promotions were handed out, Merrill did not receive one. Her boss told her that he appreciated her hard work, but she lacked the people skills necessary for the job. Recognizing that she needed a break, he suggested that she take a few weeks off and get some rest. "We'll reevaluate your progress next year," he said.

Merrill was devastated and sank into a deep depression. It was because of the depression and she returned to talk to me. I told her that her failure to receive the promotion wasn't the end of the world. "You must take more time to live and enjoy yourself," I said. "It's fine to work hard, but you're stressed to the breaking point. I'm sorry you didn't get the promotion. I know you must be very disappointed." I let this sink in, then went on, "Sometimes situations that seem devastating turn out in retrospect to be very helpful. You're being given an opportunity to reevaluate your job situation. Do you really want to continue living the way you have been? You're a nervous wreck, and you've forgotten how to have fun."

Merrill stared at me angrily, then said as though she hadn't heard me, "I cannot believe my boss said that I lacked people skills. I just try to make everyone do the best job they can. What's so bad about that? If I work hard, so should they!"

"Not everyone has the same abilities and the same capacities," I said. "You mustn't expect everyone to feel the same way you do about work. Yes, it's good to want to do a good job, but it sounds to me as if you're too hard on people. One can be firm and kind at the same time."

"I planned to make general manager before I was twenty-eight years old, and now it's not going to happen," she said.

"Why twenty-eight?" I asked.

"I've always set time goals for myself. I finished college at the age of twenty-one, grad school at twenty-three. I always felt that I could do things faster than other people. It's important to me."

"That's unfortunate for you, Merrill. Life can throw curveballs; you must be able to adapt. You mustn't live within such strict guidelines. You'll never have any peace in your life if you keep yourself totally goal-oriented. How about your spiritual development?"

"I don't know what you mean. I'm not interested in any particular church," she said.

I explained that I meant service and thinking of others. She half listened, obviously uninterested in this part of the discussion. When our time was up, Merrill left, saying angrily that she would get the promotion the next time. Nothing would stop her. She wanted to have the power that the promotion would bring with it. All she had to do was work harder. But I knew that Merrill would never gain any *real* power from her relentless ambition. It was a tragedy, but she would have many more lifetimes to learn the lesson.

PARENTS AND POWER

There is no chance involved in the birth process. The soul projecting a new personality incarnates into an environment that is needed to balance karma and promote growth. There's heavy karma involved in raising children. Parents are responsible for teaching their children right and wrong, because karmically they chose to raise them. It's the duty of good parents to help their children become strong, balanced, kind people. Parents must teach their children communication. Parents must be available to observe, listen to, discuss, and direct their children. A child's small act of cruelty, left ignored, can boomerang into a large character flaw. Parents have a very powerful karmic position in the lives of their children.

Tom: The Apple Doesn't Fall Far from the Tree

My client, Annie, has a six-year-old son, Tom. On the first day of school an eight-year-old boy stole Tom's lunch. Tom was upset, but he felt powerless to fight back and didn't want to tell the teacher because he was afraid the older kid would hurt him. He finally discussed the problem with his mother, who tried to explain why some kids are bullies. It's sad but true: Kids, as well as adults, can be mean. They act with cruelty because it makes them feel powerful when they're picking on someone weaker.

Annie wrote Tom's teacher a note alerting the school about the bully's behavior. The teacher was grateful for this information and taught the older boy that his actions would have consequences. He has stopped grabbing lunches. Tom is no longer afraid to go to school.

You've Got to Be Carefully Taught

"We allow others to create bad karma if we give people the power to torment us," Lawrence said, and he used this fable to illustrate his point:

> Once upon a time there was a lion who ate every person he came across. A great Master approached the lion and said, "Why are you eating people who aren't harming you? You are doing something very wrong, and you will pay for this. You are creating bad karma around yourself." The Master returned to see the lion a few months later. He was surprised to see that the animal was badly hurt and bleeding. "What has happened to you, lion?" he asked. "You told me to stop eating people because it was bad, so I did as you told me," the lion answered. "I never said that you shouldn't growl and scare them," the Master replied. "Now your complacency has caused you harm, and you allowed all those people to create negative karma because you let them beat you."

The lion's story is applicable to our own society. Children must be taught how to protect themselves. We must show them right from wrong. We must listen carefully when they let out even a small roar. We must teach them that teasing is cruel and unacceptable and to take a stand when they witness injustice. We must take personal responsibility for the karmic behavior in our society. Indifference will not protect us from the effects of society's karmic boomerangs.

The current horror of school shootings is a sobering indictment of our society's karma. Take out your *Power of Karma* Journal and answer the following questions:

1. Am I doing anything that would make another person feel helpless, powerless, desperate, or alienated?
2. Am I afraid to speak up when I suspect trouble because I think it's not my business?
3. Am I accepting the moral responsibility to report any incident that might have dangerous or even tragic results—no matter how insignificant it may seem?
4. Do I let people know they can talk to me if they need to?
5. Is my personal conduct on the level of integrity that could serve as a model to others?

Study your answers, and if you need to adjust your behavior, *do so immediately.* Don't waste time complaining or making excuses. These are life-and-death issues, and there's no time for procrastination. This exercise is beneficial not only to ourselves but for society at large.

History is the record of the human struggle. It is the sum

total of karmic actions and corresponding reactions. Throughout the ages we have been asked to take a stand for good or for evil. This struggle continues, and with each day new history is born. We can be remembered for our greatness as a society that protected the weak, worked in harmony for the good of all, and promoted the ideals of free choice and personal responsibility. Let us not be remembered as a selfish, narcissistic, venal society. The choice is ours to make. The future is in our hands. Today's action is tomorrow's history.

Take out two *purple* index cards and write:

1. History is a record of the human struggle.
2. Today's action is tomorrow's history.

Power Play: The Story of Ruth

My friend Ruth was outraged that her boyfriend had ended their six-year relationship. Yet she'd repeatedly told me that she was unhappy and that she herself planned to end the affair. She was outraged that he had taken the power out of her hands by calling it quits first. "How dare he make this decision without discussing it with me? I wanted to be the one who told him it was over!" she screamed.

I'd never seen Ruth behave like this. I told her she was acting irrationally. She then turned her anger on me. "How could you know how it feels to be dumped?"

"Ruth, everyone has experienced rejection at one time or another. Don't forget—you *wanted* to break up," I answered.

"But I didn't want *him* to do it. Now he thinks that it was all his idea. Everyone will think that he had the upper hand in this relationship," she replied.

Ruth was freaked out because she felt powerless. I tried to reason with her, telling her to be grateful that she didn't have to take on the bad karma for hurting her boyfriend. "He probably initiated the end because he felt it was coming. You're not heartbroken," I told her. "Your ego is bruised."

It took time for Ruth to understand that her basic problem was her need to be in control. She didn't love her boyfriend—she loved to be in the driver's seat. Then I gave her tools to help her develop the real power that comes from self-knowledge and love. I told Ruth to take out a *purple* index card and write:

Self-knowledge is the beginning of power.

"Keep this with you and look at it. Use it as a bookmark," I said.

"What do you mean by 'self-knowledge,' Mary?" Ruth asked.

"To know ourselves is to acknowledge our strengths and weaknesses and how to control them. Once we've achieved such self-knowledge, we can begin to master and enjoy personal relationships. An inflated ego can be a major stumbling block to a truly gratifying relationship with another, because we may deny the other's strength or deny our own weakness. This can lead to a "power struggle"—always wanting to have the upper hand. Most people haven't taken the time to examine their true selves, and the result is confusion, anger, and false pride. And that's why self-knowledge is indeed the beginning of power," I answered.

I then instructed Ruth to take out another *purple* index card, write down this prayer, and use it whenever she felt powerless:

I ask my higher self to help me to gain the power to over-come any barriers that keep me from personal happiness.

I told her to take out her *Power of Karma* Journal and write across the top of a page:

THE WRITING-ON-THE-WALL EXERCISE

I instructed Ruth to draw a vertical line down the middle of a page, creating two columns. In the left column she was to list at least ten times in the last three months of the relationship that she'd been happy. In the right column she was to list all the things in the relationship that had made her unhappy. Ruth spent a good deal of time writing in her journal. When she showed it to me, there were only three entries in the left-hand column. But there were forty-one entries in the right-hand column.

Well, this exercise showed Ruth that the writing was on the wall. There had been no love lost, just an ego problem. This exercise is very useful to help us examine and get at the true nature of any part of our lives. By knowing ourselves *and* our motivations, we can begin to acquire the power of decisiveness.

I'm happy to report that this inner work helped Ruth attract a new, harmonious personal relationship. She no longer wages power struggles. The joy of being involved with an equal partner has made Ruth a much kinder, more aware person. She keeps her index cards with her and has made copies of them for many of her friends. Ruth has reaped the good karma of a wonderful relationship and also the karmic joy that comes from helping others. Her motivation continues to be a quest for a deeper understanding of her own life and of all life. She is a great example of how powerful self-knowledge is in helping us to earn a better, brighter future.

MAYA

Sadly, many people confuse love with their need to be in charge, control or possess another person. This isn't real power. It is *maya*, a Sanskrit word that means "illusion," or "misconception."

Lawrence once illustrated maya in this way:

There is an ancient story of a man who is walking down the street and jumps in fear as he sees a snake. He moves closer and sees it's not a snake but a piece of rope. He laughs at himself when he realizes that he reacted to something that wasn't real.

Lawrence says that real power is charged with integrity. It is not based on fear, intimidation, domination, or force. It is rooted in fairness, honor, decency, tolerance, and self-esteem. It is rooted also in detachment.

Take out a *purple* index card and write:

Real power is rooted in detachment.

THE POWER OF DETACHMENT

Over the years many people have told me they define detachment as acting with indifference. At its worst, being detached, they say, is being totally devoid of feeling. Some think it's having a "loser's" mentality—lacking ambition, unconcerned with acquisition. It's a common misconception that one can't live in the world and be detached, that to be detached one must live in a cloister, take a vow of poverty, renounce all relationships, or live alone in the woods. In actuality, to live in the world *and* be detached is a much greater test of one's character than is removing oneself from all worldly temptations.

Detachment does not mean indifference: it means *not expecting.* Expectation causes disappointment when things do not turn out the way we want them to. Detachment is the ability to accept what is and not ask "what if?" If we learn to love everyone and every part of our lives with detachment, we will not be bound by our own desires. We will love for the total joy of doing so. It is the greatest freedom anyone can aspire to earn. And it is a powerful feeling to be liberated from the torments of *stuff*. Wealth, power, fame, relationships—all these come and go. A person who acquires the ability to be detached will accept the gifts and bear the losses. Detachment doesn't mean we have to live in the streets with a beggar's bowl. In fact, the beggar may be much more attached than the millionaire. It's a state of mind. We must be able to live *with or without* things and remain in a state of inner balance whichever way the wind blows.

Let's face it, we're all burdened with stuff. What is stuff? It's the opposite of detachment—attachments of many kinds. Here are some synonyms for stuff: belongings, personal effects, junk, baggage, trappings, gear, nonsense, poppycock, and hogwash. Add the word "shirt" after "stuffed" and you'll find a conceited, pompous, jerk. If you stuff a ballot box, you fix an election. And if you stuff yourself with food, you become a glutton. So "stuff" is a very large word with myriad meanings, none of which we need to have, to be, or to do. Don't you think it's just common sense that we'd be happier if we would lighten our load of *stuff*? This is the first step toward learning the joy of living a life of detachment.

EXERCISE: LIGHTENING OUR LOAD OF STUFF

Take out your *Power of Karma* Journal and make a list of stuff you would like to get rid of: physical, emotional, and/or spiritual.

It's well known that physical clutter can be a sign of emotional or spiritual overload, but not always. There are people who can live in a place that appears messy to some but is fine with the inhabitant. Don't judge anyone else's choice of living style.

Let's say you're a person who never lets go of an injustice that has been done to you. That is emotional stuff, and it can take away your power, leaving you drained. *Write this down:* **I will let go of the past.**

Another type of clutter is an angry mind. Some people tend to go through life with deep feelings of having been treated unfairly. *Write this down:* **I'm not a victim and will not act like one.**

This is a broad exercise, because "stuff" means different things to different people. Once you've decided what you'd like to rid yourself of, *do it!* When you have accomplished the first step, go to the second one. Then the third, and so on. This is a life's work. Don't defeat yourself by thinking it's impossible. Just start to lighten your load little by little. Step by step. In time you will see the results of your labor. Think of how a drawer full of papers you don't need looks after you've discarded the clutter; that is how your mind will feel in time. That is true detachment.

ANOTHER TYPE OF DETACHMENT

If you're painting a picture and all you're thinking about is how it will be received by others and how much money it will bring, you'll probably be miserable and ultimately dissatisfied with your work. Now, if you do the art for the joy of creation and let the chips fall where they may, you will love what you're doing. You'll be free to enjoy the process. If you sell your painting, that's great. Enjoy the money. If no one buys it, hang it on your wall and try again—the next one could be even better. This is the freedom of living in the moment, detached from the uncertainty of the "what if?" Remember, if it's your karma to sell your artwork, write a great book, marry a wonderful person, or acquire wealth, you *will* do it. The key to living a balanced life is to follow your dreams, to love and learn, but remain detached. All things pass, while the spirit remains.

THE POWER OF PERSONAL RESPONSIBILITY

Sam's Ego Gets Canned

Sam arrived for a session with me feeling angry and depressed. He'd just been fired for the third time in a year. He insisted on blaming karma from a past life (which *might* have been the case), but his problem was obviously active in this one. Sam projected an arrogance that made people want to stay away from him.

He refused to accept any personal responsibility for his behavior. I saw and pointed out definite incidents in the workplace that had caused him to be fired: his rudeness to his bosses, his lack of respect for other workers, his habitual tardiness, and his relentless need to be the center of attention. Sam's mantra was "I am a victim . . . I am a victim . . . a victim."

I predicted that he'd be fired again unless he changed his behavior. Sam said that I was wrong, that it was a past-life issue, and that he was a victim of karma.

"Sam, I'm honored to be with such an expert on karma," I said facetiously. "I don't see this as a karmic issue, but rather a question of character. You have the power to change your job history. Stop acting like a victim and grow up," I said to him as he was leaving.

He returned to see me one year later, having lost two more jobs. "Okay," he said, "maybe I *am* doing something wrong." It took the loss of five jobs in two years for Sam to face the music. Duh—he was *clearly* doing something wrong.

"Sam, you fought with your bosses over trivial matters. I see that your last boss wanted you to hand in your expenses weekly. You refused, called him stupid, and told him you'd hand them in monthly," I said. He told me he was startled at the precision of my psychic information. "Sam, your ego, not your karma, got you canned. The acceptance of the truth is the beginning of real power," I said. "You have the ability to modify your behavior in order to redirect your work life from chaos to balance."

I had told him write the following on a *purple* index card and carry it with him at all times:

Real power is based on integrity.

I also told him to write in his *Power of Karma* Journal:

1. Job history—how many and how long?
2. Honest reasons for losing the jobs.

Sam spent a great deal of time writing out the details of his job history. He realized he had to face and conquer his own bad behavior. He focused morning and evening on changing his point of view from that of victim to that of victor. Sam kept copious notes on his progress. It wasn't easy, but he prevailed. A year later he came for another session and was positively glowing. He reported he'd been at his current job for ten months and was very happy. I was delighted to predict that I saw no work-related problems for Sam as long as he continued on his current karmic path.

I impressed upon him the need to keep working on refining his behavior. He mustn't let down his guard. He assured me that the new feeling of being in control of his behavior was terrific. It was the "real power" we'd discussed during our first meeting. "I like living with the 'good karma' I've earned," he said with a smile as he left that day.

THE MISUSE OF POWER

There are people who love to wield power in a small way and those who love to wield it in a large way. Love of power plays havoc with reason. History has proven that power can corrupt. Many famous people, dominated by their lust for power, are destroyed by their egotism and unquenchable thirst for personal gain. But you don't have to be famous to destroy your life with your unbalanced pursuit of power. It can happen to anyone. There is heavy karma connected to the use and misuse of power. So make sure that you can handle the responsibility that comes with power before you attract it.

THE POWER OF THOUGHT

Your whole life and all aspects of your being are direct outcomes of your thinking. Thought is everything; there is nothing without it. Our whole life, as well as our past lives, is the physical realization of thoughts. Every aspect of our being is a direct outcome of our thinking. It's unfathomable just how powerful this process is. It's not only actions but thoughts that create karma. A painting is the thought of an image that is put on canvas. A musical composition is thought turned into structured sound. This book you are reading is thought turned into language represented by symbols that express the language.

We must learn to guard our thoughts as the sentinel guards his post. Do not allow yourself to become lax in your thinking. You must learn to discipline your thoughts until you're able to think positively with no effort. Negative thinking causes one to live a life that is out of balance, which in turn creates bad karma. What is negative thinking? It is any thought of ill will, greed, despair, anger turned upon oneself or another person, self-pity, or revenge. Positive thoughts are those that are loving, kind, constructive, productive, and forgiving.

In order to produce good karma, we must practice proper thinking. We all have encountered people whom we'd call negative. You know the type—they're never satisfied. If the sky is blue, it's not blue enough. If they get a job promotion, it isn't senior enough. If they're given a compliment, it isn't the right one. These poor souls are not aware that they're being negative. For some reason this has become their modus operandi, so they continue to see the glass as half empty rather than half full, wondering why *they* feel unfulfilled.

Not all cases of the "negatives" are as extreme, but all forms of this type of thinking will cause nothing but trouble. I'm not suggesting that we all live in denial—everybody has problems and concerns. But we must learn to detach, acknowledge our troubles and then deal with them to the best of our ability. Don't allow the blues to coopt your power! Doesn't it make sense that if you live your life cloaked in an aura of negativity, you'll attract negativity? Remember the boomerang?

Sally Sings the Blues

Sally was mugged late one afternoon. When she called me, she was quite hysterical. She wanted to know why it was her karma to have been mugged. "There must have been twenty people walking down the street, and this mugger singled me out. What did I do in a past life to deserve this?" she asked tearfully.

"Before you blame a past life, we'd better examine this one. Do you remember what you were thinking right before this happened?" I asked.

She sighed and said, "I'd been having a terrible day. I was feeling angry and resentful about my job. I was thinking how much I hate my boss and how I wish she'd get fired. Now that I think about it, I was so angry I didn't notice the guy following me. I was so wrapped up in my rage I wasn't even looking where I was going."

"Sally, thank goodness you're okay, but don't ignore this valuable lesson. Being wrapped up in negative thinking can be dangerous," I replied.

"You're right," she admitted. "I've got to get control of my emotions. My boss is fine. *I'm* the one who was robbed."

"You must begin with changing your thinking, and the emotions will follow. It's always thought that urges us into noble acts or gives rise to devastating endeavors. The thought is the match. Once it is lit by the emotions, it creates fire. You choose how to use the flame. It can be the fire of passion to serve, or it can become a destructive wildfire," I explained.

She thanked me for my time and for helping her to see that she could change her karma by redirecting her thinking. She wanted to know how to get started on her new thinking regime. "Well, the first step is to replace anger with empathy," I said. I gave her this meditation practice.

MEDITATION FOR EMPATHY

The concept of empathy is very important. It means the ability to understand the way another person feels. You may not agree, but the point is to be compassionate. You must take time to concentrate on the other person—even if you dislike her—and force yourself to see her merits and not her shortcomings.

Sit in a comfortable place where you will not be interrupted. Let your thoughts flow freely. Now envision your boss in the mind's eye. Don't allow yourself to hold on to anger or hatred. These negative feelings will hurt you, because they destroy your peace of mind. Think about what may be making your so-called enemy unhappy. Then project loving thoughts. Just do this, and your attitude will begin to change. This transformation will make you a more positive person, causing good karma to come into your life with greater ease.

The power to see another person's point of view is real power. This exercise should be done as often as you can. It takes only a few minutes, and you can do it almost anywhere. Every time you feel anger toward another person creeping into your thinking, stop, breathe, and redirect your thoughts toward understanding. This will work in all areas of your life: work, home, anyplace that your thoughts can make you go negative, thus causing you to attract negative feelings into your life.

THE POWER OF THE WORD

Words, like thoughts, are alive. Once something is said, it can't be recalled. If you hurt someone with your words, the person may forgive you, but the damage has been done. How many times have you been embarrassed by putting your foot in your mouth? Many heartbreaking or tragic mistakes could be avoided if we'd only think before we speak.

If you want to live in the light of good karma, you must not be judgmental or critical. Too many people spend their time and energy judging their neighbors and criticizing the deeds of their fellow beings. If we all would take a moment to try to understand the nature and behavior of the people we encounter, there would be a lot less thoughtless judgment and unnecessary pain. This takes patience. There is power in patience.

It may take great self-control to keep quiet and not stand in judgment of another's action, but try helping instead of judging. Helping, in its true sense, is *not* interfering. Only in cases where you feel that someone might be in danger should you act in a manner that could be perceived as interference. You create very bad karma if you allow a tragedy to occur because you didn't speak up.

Remember, if you hear a cry for help, it's your karma to answer it. You mustn't think, *It's his karma to be attacked, so I'll just ignore it.* Do anything in your power to avert harm. In many cases a few words could make the difference between life and death.

Lawrence never uses words gratuitously. He instructs but never judges. His nature is to point out a problem in order to to help resolve it. He can be tough, but never cruel. Lawrence is motivated only by the desire to serve everyone he meets. He really does have the patience of a saint. I, on the other hand, have a great deal to learn in the patience department.

Lawrence always smiles and says, "Little by little, my child. If you pressure yourself to be more patient, you are losing the battle before it is fought."

There is no point wasting energy or castigating ourselves for making mistakes. This type of mental exercise causes the bad karma of negativity, and it's hard to turn it around. Just be! Aspire to do the best with whatever is presented to you. A sense of humor will serve you unfailingly. It takes time to learn the art of patience, and you have plenty of time. And remember, words can wound. Slander is negative, and nothing positive can ever come from it.

All About Eve

My friend Diane is a fashion stylist. She had a secretary named Eve. The first time I met Eve, I felt a very negative vibration surrounding her—her aura was a burnt orange color that showed a jealous streak. This girl would tell people that Diane had said things about them that weren't true. I warned Diane that I saw trouble brewing—I'd called, left messages with Eve, and my calls were never returned. I know Diane's character, so I persisted until I reached her personally.

Diane confronted Eve, and Eve played dumb. "I thought that I gave you Mary T.'s messages. I'm so sorry" was her reply. Diane let it pass. She told me that she couldn't bear the thought of hiring a new person, as it was a lot of work to train someone.

"That which is easiest isn't always best. Your secretary is bad news. She'll end up hurting you and your business," I warned her.

Time passed, and Diane noticed that quite a few of her clients hadn't called in a while. She phoned two of her longstanding clients and was amazed to hear that Eve had told them not to call anymore. These clients went on to report that Eve had told them she'd charge them less to work with her. She hinted that Diane was overcharging and double billing. Diane fired Eve that day. But it took time to find out just how much damage had been done to her business. Diane took charge and was able to get back most of her clients. Still shocked by Eve's behavior, Diane called me in tears and asked, "Why did she do this to me? What did I do to her? Is this a past-life problem?"

"It's a clear-cut case of present-life jealousy. There's no rational reason for jealousy. Stop trying to find one. Just be more careful in the future to whom you trust your business." I paused to gauge her reaction.

"I tried to warn you, and I'm sure some of your other friends did as well. But you wouldn't listen to any of us. Diane, it's difficult to accept that the only reason for a person's behavior is jealousy. We always think that we must have done something to make a person act in an evil way. Some people are just rotten eggs. Eve will never be happy, because she's living in a jealous hole. She's more dangerous to herself than to anyone else. Jealousy always boomerangs and causes the initiator heartbreak and tragedy."

We learned that Eve got a new job but lost it within weeks. She spoke badly about Diane to the wrong person (a man who had known and respected Diane for twenty years). Eve's boyfriend dumped her with no warning, and she lost the lease to her apartment. Eve brought nothing but bad karma upon herself by her own behavior and bogus use of power. Boomerang!

Diane reaped a bit of negative karma because she was too lazy to get a new secretary when she got the first warning. She's doing fine now because she's a great lady with a lot of integrity who got back on track once she'd acknowledged the situation.

Power and the love of power are not the same thing. An altruistic, spiritual teacher may possess great power, but he doesn't love it, so he never abuses it. The selfish individual who loves power desires to control others. A selfless person who owns power controls himself.

Here's an exercise that's a practical antidote for ridding yourself of the bad karma reaped from anger, disdain, or intolerance.

EXERCISE: TRAFFIC CONTROL

Let's say that you're stuck in traffic. Instead of becoming angry and frustrated over something you can't control, use this time to concentrate on compassion and tolerance. Just focus your thinking on these two positive vibes. Keep repeating these words in your mind—*compassion* and *tolerance*—with conviction. The bad karma reaped from anger and negativity will vanish, and positive karma will accrue.

Every one of us has a few minutes every day when we're busy getting somewhere by car, subway, bus, train, or foot. This is a perfect time to meditate, and it will set a positive tone for the rest of the day. Just look at the people around you and send them loving thoughts. This simple yet powerful, positive process will create a radiant energy force around you, a force that will attract only good karma to you.

Now, *that's* real power!

Take out five *purple* index cards and write:

1. There is power in patience.
2. Do anything in your power to avert harm. This creates good karma.
3. A selfless person who owns power controls himself.
4. If you hear a cry for help, it's your karma to answer it.
5. The power to see another person's point of view is real power.

7. Karma and Balance

If we examine life, the concept of balance has infinite meaning; it governs our lives even if we aren't aware of it. Balance in health, family, finances, work, and all relationships in "living life"—this is the key for stability and harmony. Balance is the ultimate reason for living numerous lives. We keep coming back to earth with our bankbook, metaphorically, in the cradle. From birth until death, over and over again, we keep track of the debits and credits until at last the bottom line of our statement shows perfect balance. At that moment we will have mastered ourselves. We won't have to reincarnate again. Think about it: We will be able to stay in the spirit world living in a state of absolute bliss. It doesn't get better than that.

However, as we've examined, most people don't see life in terms of balance. They ignore its existence, break all its rules, and then complain about the cards they were dealt, when in fact *they* were the ones who stacked the deck that created the boomerang of negative karma. When viewed in light of balance, doesn't it make sense that it's wise to master—balance—our behavior and our emotions to the best of our ability? Once we do, we can channel our energies into finding the most direct route to happiness, which is, of course, a balanced life enhanced by nothing but good karma.

THE GIFT OF THE LYRE

One day, out of the blue, Lawrence called and asked me to meet him in Quebec City, at the Château Frontenac. We sat together in the hotel's charming restaurant and talked for hours. He was very pleased that my psychic work was going so well. We discussed my last book, *Life After Death,* in great detail. He wanted to know how I was progressing with this book, *The Power of Karma.* "You must look deeply into your own life's journey, and that knowledge will guide you. I have a gift that should serve as an inspiration to you."

He closed his eyes and sat quietly, as if he were in a state of prayer. He held this deep concentration for maybe a minute, then clapped his hands. A metal object fell onto the table in front of me, which he'd manifested through the power of his mind. He saw my hesitation and said, "You may pick it up."

I held in my hand an exceptionally beautifully designed pin made of sterling and gold. In the center was a lyre (harp) atop two trumpets. A long piece of sheet music was woven through the strings of the instrument. On either side of the lyre was a six-petaled flower. A circlet of leafy branches formed a perfect border. Lawrence moved the candle closer to me so I would clearly see the details of this treasure. The light flickering upon this beautiful piece added to its astonishing beauty. It looked Victorian, but I wasn't certain as to the exact age.

I was transfixed, staring at the lyre. Lawrence broke the silence. "Think deeply about the significance of the lyre pin. It holds the answer to that which you've spent a lifetime seeking. You have found your philosophy—your grail—though you've never put a name to it. Take your treasure back to New York and unravel the mystery of the lyre. Once you've discovered its meaning, you will have the ending to *The Power of Karma*." We parted outside the dining room. As I walked toward my suite, I pinned Lawrence's gift next to my heart.

THE DISCOVERY OF HARMONY

Upon my return to New York I began to research the history of the lyre. Having studied singing since childhood, I had a basic knowledge of music history. I remembered pictures of angels playing lyres. Because I'm of Irish descent, the Celtic image of the lyre also came to mind. I knew that Orpheus, the god of the underworld, played a lyre, as did his father, Apollo, the god of prophecy and music. Lawrence had once told me that the "lyre of Apollo" was a seven-stringed instrument that symbolized the mysteries of spiritual initiation. But it was Pythagoras, credited with the discovery of the diatonic scale, who ultimately gave me the key to the mystery of the lyre.

There is a story that one day as Pythagoras was meditating upon harmony, he passed a shop where men were pounding on an anvil. As he listened to the sounds of the workmen and noticed the variations of pitch, he, with his mathematical genius, discovered the law of harmonics. I recalled the history of Pythagoras, and suddenly a light went on in my head. He'd declared that a soul could be purified from any irrational or negative influences by solemn songs played on the lyre. The lyre was the symbol of harmony and balance!

The trumpets at the base of the lyre were sounded to awaken people on many levels. In this case they were alerting us to the power of harmony to balance all parts of our lives. Flowers, the symbol of beauty, represent spiritual unfolding and attainment. The flowers on the pin were in perfect balance on each side of the lyre. The branches, from the tree of life, encircled the lyre. The circle is the symbol of the universal God force, which has neither beginning nor end.

As I studied the lyre pin, everything became crystal clear. Harmony was the only possible answer for achieving balance in life. Lawrence had been giving me clues to this puzzle ever since we'd first met. He wanted me to know that harmony is the key that opens the door to a life of health, love, security, and, most of all, balance. All my life I'd been searching for something without putting a name to it. Now, through the clue of the lyre, I had found the magic word that expressed the balance of all things in nature—harmony. It was music to my ears.

KARMA AND WORK

"I've never known what I really wanted to do." "I've never had a job that made me happy." "I hate work. It's meaningless." "I don't know why I keep getting fired." "I'm a workaholic." These are just a few examples of things I've heard—and continue to hear—from my clients. Without harmony in our work there is little hope for a life of balance.

There are people who are "born" writers, doctors, lawyers, bankers, bartenders, farmers, truckers, mothers, artists, and such. These people know from childhood what they want to do with their lives. They appear to have been incarnated with this knowledge.

Not everyone is so certain. Most people have to search in order to find a job or profession that makes them feel good. Any work performed with dignity and integrity is noble labor. We know that our every action returns to us as a reaction; our actions then act on other people and theirs on us. It would be practical to aspire to love whatever you are doing, even if it's done while waiting to find something more suitable. Any act of love brings happiness, and this results in good karma.

Passion for work isn't always an innate gift. It can be acquired by finding a way to love your particular type of service. This can be any line of work. You don't have to be a minister, doctor, therapist, teacher, nun, or nurse in order to feel you are serving others. All that is needed is the desire to do the best job you possibly can. We spend a great deal of our lives working. Shouldn't we try our best to discover work that gives us a sense of joy and accomplishment? This is a major factor in our pursuit of a balanced life. A life in which every day you have to debit your karma account because of anger, laziness, resentment, or boredom is tragic because it's wasteful. And waste produces bad karma.

So let's take out four *yellow* index cards and write:

1. All work performed in the spirit of harmony promotes balance.
2. I can and will find work that I delight in.
3. A life in which every day you have to debit your karma account is tragic because it is wasteful.
4. Waste produces bad karma.

Dan Jumps Ship

Dan became a lawyer because the first son of every generation was expected to do so. It was a family tradition; no discussion—case closed. Dan had tried once to talk to his mother about his fear that the law wouldn't make him happy. She patted him on the head and said, "Don't be silly, dear, everyone in the family is happy." Not having the courage to rock the boat, he went off to Harvard and graduated at the top of his class. Dan was hired by an excellent firm, where he worked for seven years, giving his all. He was liked and respected by his colleagues and was being considered for a partnership. In terms of the prevailing worldview, Dan had "made it." In reality, he was bordering on despair when he came to see me.

"Mary T., can you explain karma to me?" he asked.

"How many days do you have, Dan? Karma is a large subject. Simply put, it means 'action.' Everything is karma—past, present, and future. Don't you want to talk about your work karma?" I smiled.

"You hit the nail on the head," he said with a touch of surprise.

"That's my job," I said.

We didn't talk about the law. I said that I knew he was a lawyer and a very successful one, but I saw his future work in a very different field. I told him I saw him living on a small island with a fishing boat. I described the island in detail and added that he would be happy and also make a very good living. Dan started to cry. All he'd ever wanted was to be a professional fisherman and live as I'd described. He talked about his sense of obligation to his family. He was confused because he thought maybe it was his karma to have to live his whole life in a profession that wasn't right for him.

"Dan, it is your karma to be part of your family. You must have the courage to tell them that you're going to pursue a career change. You must be able to handle their reaction. You are a remarkable person, and I know that you'll find a way to deal with them kindly but firmly. Dan, if a man is afraid of the dark, does he have to remain that way for his whole life, or could he through knowledge overcome his fear? It was your karma to become a lawyer, and now it's your karma to find the best way to leave the law," I told him.

Dan knew it would be no walk in the park. He'd have to initiate great changes in order to achieve his dream. But he was willing to do whatever was needed to find the balance he so desperately missed in his life. I predicted he'd be able to change professions within three years.

Dan returned to see me two and a half years later, utterly transformed. He had done the hard work; he had faced his family and stood firm, knowing he'd made the right decision. He made plans and worked hard at the law until he could afford to leave and start his new business.

I knew he was going to be very happy. He'd shaped his future through strategy, hard work, and clear vision. His family didn't understand, but they were coping. Dan remained kind but incorruptible. He knew that his karma had changed because he'd changed his actions. He didn't blame karma for the years he'd spent as an unfulfilled lawyer. He embraced the good karma that came from recognizing the work that would balance his life, and he enjoyed every step on the path that led to the fulfillment of his dream.

Dan's steps may help you. Write them in your *Power of Karma* Journal:

1. Make a plan for your future.
2. Accept that it will take hard work.
3. Keep your vision clear.
4. Remain kind but incorruptible.

Peter Knocks on Wood

When Peter arrived, he was depressed because he had no passion for any type of work. He wasn't lazy and didn't expect life to be easy, but he was approaching forty and felt useless. Peter had been a stockbroker, a software salesman, and the editor of a small magazine. He'd graduated college with a business degree because he couldn't think of anything better to major in. I'd met many Peters in my work—people who embarked on whatever career presented itself because they had no real passion for any particular profession. "I thought you might be able to tell me what I was born to do in this life," he said as he sat down. He looked at me in a respectful yet almost pleading manner. His eyes were kind, yet sad at the same time. I could feel his pain.

As I sat looking at Peter, I felt a strong pressure against my forehead. It alerted me to concentrate on the Akashic records. I focused my eyes to the corner of my living room and saw a very clear past-life picture of Peter. "You have a gift for making wood furniture," I said. "You lived in a small German village about eight hundred years ago. You learned the art of making wood pieces from a wonderful old man who was known for the excellence of his craftsmanship. The problem was that you were female in that life, so no one would let you pursue your dream." I paused, forcing myself to hold the picture for a moment longer. "The old man is telling you he's sorry, but people are stubborn and they can't imagine a girl doing a man's job. He assures you that one day you'll be a master furniture maker." As quickly as it came, the picture evaporated.

I looked over at Peter, and he appeared stunned. "I used to dream about making church pews when I was little," he told me. "The only class in high school I ever loved was shop. I made a table and won a prize. I remember telling my father how much I loved woodworking. He laughed at me and said 'That's a hobby, not a profession.' He wouldn't even discuss the possibility that I might want to make a living that way." Peter's eyes teared up. He sat lost in thought and then asked, "Do you really think that I could make a living doing something I love?"

"Absolutely." I paused and then continued. "Within a year you could be working at a job that you'd find unbelievably fulfilling. Look for a cabinetmaker who needs an apprentice. This will be your way into a business you'll love."

After Peter left that day, something Lawrence once told me came to mind: "The childhood is, in most cases, a prominent cause of a person's formation or malformation. It has an important place in most human behavior, in most reaction, in most emotions. Accordingly, the tree will grow how it is rooted, straight or not."

Peter's father had been very cruel to laugh and dismiss his son's aspirations and talent. He created karmic chaos for Peter and bad karma for himself.

I received a note from Peter a year after our session. He'd found an apprenticeship, as I had predicted. He was so talented that within six months he began to earn money through his work. To say that Peter is over the moon is putting it lightly. His work karma changed from frustration to elation.

I don't always get these clear pictures of someone's past life. Karma makes that decision, not me. It was Peter's karma to be given the information from the Akashic records. It was my karma to be able to give it to him. Psychic phenomena can be startling and titillating, but so what? The important thing is what a person does with the information. Peter took the knowledge and with faith and hard work reshaped his life into a happier one. He confirmed, by his actions, that he'd earned the right to have a past-life reading. He was able to overcome his father's negativity and go ahead with work that promotes beauty and harmony. He's living proof that life does begin at forty.

Take a *yellow* index card and write:

A tree will grow as it is rooted.

KARMA, TALENT, AND THE BIG TIME

It's been my privilege to meet many talented people—artists, dancers, writers, decorators, actors, and musicians. Many of them are earning their living through their art, although most are not. Having worked in music and the theater, I feel very protective of artists. I understand the frustration of rejection slips from publishers, closed doors to agents' offices, unanswered phone calls, the seeming impossibility of being seen or heard by a director. It's true that many gifted people are unable to pay the rent through their work. It's also true that while many are called, few seem to be chosen.

Karma plays a huge role in whether a person becomes famous, wealthy, admired, respected, or simply able to make a living through his or her talent. It takes many lifetimes to perfect an art. The process can be painful, unbalancing, and depressing if the karma effect isn't understood. Envy, sour grapes, and the oft-heard mantra "It's not fair" are dangerous reactions for people who are pursuing their creative goals. These negative feelings will only boomerang on the originator. I believe that we can learn from studying the lives of great artists who have suffered yet left the world a more beautiful place because of their gifts. Great artists are spiritual messengers.

I am reminded of Vincent van Gogh. Until he was twenty-seven, he studied to become a Protestant minister. He failed to become one because he refused to take a test in Latin. He was proficient in four languages, Latin being one of them. However, he felt that Latin wouldn't help people because nobody spoke it, so he left the church. He decided he could more effectively impart his message of spirituality through painting.

Van Gogh was a man who combined the Eastern and Western ways of thinking far before it was fashionable to do so. He painted the Japanese way with the Western touch, and he studied the religions of the East in order to better balance his painting style. In 1888 he painted himself as a Buddhist monk. He had great passion for his work but sold only one painting before his death at the age of thirty-seven. His passion and his extraordinary personal vision drove him to insanity. Yet he left us with awe-inspiring works of art. It was his karma to depart the earth without being able to enjoy the fruits of his labor.

Rebecca: Always a Trooper

Rebecca called to tell me that she had just landed a part in a Broadway play. She'd been auditioning for seven years, and this was her first big break. She would finally be able to quit her job waiting tables and work as a full-time actress. She was ecstatic, and I was thrilled for her. When I had first met her five years earlier, she was working very hard, acting part-time for little or no pay, and, like many other actors, earned her living at any kind of job she could find. But she never complained. She always remained confident that one day she would be a full-time actress.

Rebecca had loved the theater all her life and had a university degree in the theater arts. She was always happy when a friend of hers got a professional job, and never once did I know of her to be envious of another's good fortune. She used to say to me, "I have been given talent, and I would like to use it to entertain people. I always feel so happy when people tell me that they enjoyed a performance of mine. I just feel good that I was able to make someone happy." She understood innately that her talent was a gift to be used to help others.

Her attitude allowed her to live each day to its fullest and keep pursuing her dream no matter how many disappointments she experienced along the way. Rebecca was secure in the knowledge that when the time came, the right role would come to her. She said that she always did her best and knew that she could do no more.

If more people viewed their work as Rebecca does, they would be much happier. It's not an uncommon experience to be treated in a rude, surly manner by an actor, writer, musician, or dancer working as a waiter in a restaurant in order to make ends meet. Such people may be taking out their frustrations, disappointments, and feelings of rejection on the easiest available target, entirely forgetting how fortunate they are to have a job that keeps them fed and housed while allowing them to study and audition. If you're in such a position, remember that if you are to have work in your chosen field, it will come to you. Meanwhile, keep yourself in the vibration of your work by studying, auditioning, and doing the best you can in all aspects of your life, including the day-to-day job that pays the bills.

Many times I have heard complaints such as the following: "I don't understand. My friend just got to town, and three days later she landed a role in a film. It's not fair! I've been auditioning for two years and haven't gotten anything."

My reply is always the same. "Your friend earned her part, or it would not have come to her. It's a matter of karma. It takes many incarnations to perfect any art. You can't know how many lifetimes your friend has been polishing her craft. Be grateful for the talent you have been given, and don't worry about the success of others. It's foolish and dangerous to judge your life against anyone else's. You will poison yourself with jealousy. All that you have earned will come to you. How does it serve you to spend your time being angry and envious? Let go of your anger and work on your craft. Enjoy your work and don't worry about the result. Just keep working in the knowledge that you have been given the talent and are thankful for the gift!"

Take out a *yellow* index card and write:

All that you have earned will come to you.

Ricky Changes the Picture

Ricky wanted to be a professional musician. He arrived for his appointment feeling defeated and dejected. He blamed the universe for keeping him from fulfilling his dream. But I saw that Ricky didn't practice his music and tended to party five nights a week. I brought this to his attention, and he admitted that he lacked discipline. I stressed that it appeared obvious that he didn't want his music enough to fight for it. "Ricky, there's no free lunch. You have to decide what your focus in life is going to be, be. You're going to have to change your lifestyle drastically if you're going to become a working musician," I said.

"It's really hard," he said petulantly.

"You aren't focused, you don't practice—you might as well admit you'd prefer to party than to be a professional musician. It's your decision. Don't blame the universe for your laziness and lack of dedication. Give yourself a break and realize that maybe you are confused about your true purpose in life. It's all right to admit that what you're seeking is too hard. You'll have other lives to try to become a working musician. Why don't you just chill out?" I told him.

This shocked Ricky. He thought about it for a minute and

then said, "I never wanted to really look at myself, but I just did, and it's not a happy picture."

"You can change the picture if you really want to, Ricky," I added. He went on to describe his childhood and how his father had told him he'd never amount to anything. Ricky hadn't realized he was living out his father's prediction. His past in *this* life was still affecting him. I stressed that he was no longer a child in need of his father's confirmation. He would have to choose to take control of his own future, or he'd continue living a frustrated, empty life.

Ricky returned to his music lessons with new focus and vigor. He forced himself to practice an hour a day; in time he found that time stretching to three hours. He rediscovered his love of music, and practice was no longer a chore. It took Ricky three years, a number of odd jobs, and a change in his lifestyle, but today he's got a great job in a band. He told me he's never been happier, and each day he feels better and better about his work. The best thing that happened was that his father came to hear him play. He told Ricky he was very proud of him. Who said that you can't teach an old dog new tricks?

Take out two *yellow* index cards and write:

1. I won't blame karma for my laziness and lack of dedication.
2. The universe is not responsible for my unfulfilled dreams. I am.

EXERCISE: IN PURSUIT OF HARMONY

The mind can't focus on two thoughts at one time. Whenever a resentful, envious, hostile, or destructive thought enters your mind, immediately replace it with the word *harmony*. Everything in life that comes from creating good karma is contained in *harmony*: health, love, security, strength, and inspiration. *Harmony* means balance.

Acquire the habit of using the word *harmony* whenever you feel fearful, insecure, lonely, or anxious. It's essential that you understand *harmony*, not just intellectually but with your whole being. Let's not forget that we're working toward putting our karmic bank accounts into complete balance. Achieving *harmony* is the most important step in that process.

For instance, before an important meeting it will calm you if you quietly say to yourself, "I am entering this meeting in harmony." Keep repeating the word *harmony* inside your head, and you will be enveloped by calm. This powerful word will keep the bad karma created by negative thinking at bay.

Meditate on *harmony*: love it, integrate it into every action, word, and thought. Keep it within you, as a type of tune, and when you are worried or afraid, take it out and hum it. Keep listening to the melody until you feel yourself moving into the rhythm of balance, into *harmony*.

ENLIGHTENMENTS

An enlightenment is an action that gradually leads us toward a more balanced way of life. Every step taken that promotes personal growth increases the light in our lives. Light increases good karma. My design to help you shape your future involves using the following enlightenments.

The Power of the Will and Strength

In order to develop your will you must have an idea of what you want in your life. You must decide upon your life purpose. Be realistic. If you're forty and have never danced in your life, you'll never be a prima ballerina—no matter how badly you want it. But if you're a secretary and desire to be an executive, you must go back to school and study. You may have to work full-time and go to school at night for a few years. Fatigue, financial worry, scheduling problems—all must be dealt with in order to achieve your desired professional goal. It won't be easy, but if you persevere, you won't fail. The fact remains that there are many things in life that aren't easy. Difficulties can be overcome with adequate willpower combined with strength. The will and strength are inseparable.

The power of the will lies in our individual skill in directing it. Anyone can achieve a greater degree of willpower. It takes determination, patience, and strength.

Don't spend your time regretting past mistakes. Make up your mind not to repeat them. If you fail, tell yourself, "I will not do this again, because it makes me unhappy." No matter how many times you have to start over, do so. We fail because we refuse to persevere. Focus on your purpose and don't waste energy beating yourself up because you blew it.

Strength comes from experience, repetition, contemplation, and emulating those who are stronger than ourselves. We must not rationalize weakness, we must fight to overcome it. Through the process of contemplation we can examine our lives and discover the reasons for past failures. We must be objective and look at our good and bad qualities without using any "filter." We all have flaws, and if we spend a few minutes each day examining ourselves, we can uncover them and work on them.

If you remain committed to your goal, the day will come when you will see the results of your labor.

Kindness

Kindness is a critical component in karmic balance. Remember the boomerang—unkind actions, thoughts, and words hurt not only their subject but the one who is unkind, even if he or she is not immediately aware of it. Lawrence counsels that we think about kindness, saying, "Think of three people in your life toward whom you've been unkind, and observe how this made you feel."

We're all human, and thus we have good and bad days. We don't necessarily intend to be unkind but sometimes it happens. People who are aware of and in touch with their feelings will feel terrible when they realize they've been unkind. It may be the mere act of snapping at your assistant because you're under pressure. In the heat of an argument you may say horrible things to a loved one. A mother can devastate a child by random acts of unkindness, and vice versa.

Take out a *yellow* index card and write:

Unkindness always creates bad karma, because it's based in selfishness.

Linda's Left Field

A client, Linda, has never gotten over her mother's saying, "Take that skirt off—you look like a tramp." Linda was fifteen and had borrowed a skirt from her girlfriend to wear to a party. It was the latest style, and Linda thought it looked great. She had been excited to show her mother the outfit and was devastated by her mom's harsh comment. Her mother's unthinking reaction came out of left field; Linda had never heard her mother speak with such cruelty.

Linda ran up to her room, cried for hours, and refused to go to the party. It turns out that her mother was angry at Linda's father but had taken her anger out on Linda. Linda still fights feelings of low self-esteem. She said to me, "Can you imagine your mother calling you a tramp? She could have told me nicely that she didn't like the skirt. I never did anything in my life that made me deserve to be labeled a tramp by my mother."

Linda's mother had to live with the fact that her words couldn't be recalled. She'd told Linda she was sorry, but the damage had been done. Boomerang. Linda is a sweet, sensitive, forgiving girl, but she still feels a sting when she thinks of those unkind words from her mother. Linda still can't let go of her pain—she hasn't learned detachment.

Parents must be aware that children learn by example. Children must be taught to be kind. Selfish, mean children usually learn their behavior in the home. Parents are often guilty about something, so they overindulge children, and this can be a great unkindness. The need to work long hours in order to support the family leaves parents little time to spend with their children. This can result in their allowing the children to be demanding and to lack common courtesy.

I often watch children playing in the park near my apartment building. It saddens me to see so many who are unwilling to share with their playmates. Many kids are just plain mean to other kids. Unless this behavior is corrected, they will grow into selfish, mean adults.

In some cases parents do everything they can to teach their child kindness and respect, and it just doesn't work. It's possible the child has a character flaw brought in from a past life. But remember, karma can be shaped. Parents should continue to educate the child to be good and thoughtful. Perseverance will, eventually have a positive effect.

As we should strive to be good to our children, so should we act toward our parents. People who put their parents into nursing homes and rarely or never visit will probably end up being treated in the same manner by their children. It's not always possible to take care of our family members in our homes. We should still be kind and loving, and visit as often as possible.

The workplace appears to be a breeding ground for unkindness. Is it so difficult to behave in a decent manner at work? A good boss can be tough while remaining humane. Hundreds of clients over the years have arrived for their sessions with me in despair over cruel treatment at work.

Here's an exercise that will help you change your workplace from one full of bad karma to one with good karmic vibes:

> You must remain kind, even if everyone else is behaving negatively. Observe how positive, thoughtful behavior rubs off on others. This isn't easy, but it is very powerful. It could, in time, make your whole work environment tolerable—even enjoyable.

Another exercise for helping us to integrate kindness into all aspects of our lives is this one:

> Think about being kind the first thing in the morning and the last thing at night. At the end of your day think about everything that happened in the last twenty-four hours. Could you have been kinder to someone? Did you observe a cruel action and do nothing about it? Are you attracting negativity because you're acting unpleasantly?

Every action we perform affects not only ourselves but everyone. We are all connected to each other. Kindness has a profound effect on the collective karma in the universe.

Patience

> Patience attains all that it strives for.
>
> —ST. TERESA OF AVILA

Patience is calmness, tranquillity, self-control, tolerance, dignity, and the ability to endure without complaint. As such, it has been called a virtue. We all are not born with a natural gift for being able to accept life's trials calmly. We tend to admire those who are able to wait for things to happen without anger, a short temper, or anxiety.

Take out a *yellow* index card and write:

Without patience life is one long lament.

We must never lose sight of the fact we have many lives, not just this one, in which to perfect ourselves. There is tremendous enjoyment in experiencing the gradual process of personal growth in any area of our lives. Whether in romance, raising our children, or developing friendships, patience is fundamental.

Take out two *yellow* index cards and write:

1. **Talents and relationships must be free to bloom in their own time.**
2. **I will not be in such a hurry that I miss the beauty of the moment.**

Respect

When we respect something or someone, we honor, admire, cherish, protect, and defend that thing or person. The world would be a better place if we all spent a few minutes each day contemplating the power of respect and acting appropriately in all aspects of our lives.

Lauren's Lament

Lauren was in despair when she came to see me. She'd dated a man for three months, and he'd suddenly stopped calling her. The night before, she'd seen him with another girl at a restaurant; he just ignored her. Lauren was in a complete state of shock and wanted to know what I "saw" about their relationship.

"I don't know why you would choose to accept such disrespect from anyone," I answered. "He obviously has little regard for you or your feelings, and I believe that it was a blessing when you ran into him."

Lauren reflected on what I'd said. "But he told me that he loved me," she almost shouted.

"Actions speak louder than words in this case, Lauren. You must not only *listen* to what people say, you must *observe* what they do. This man showed a lack of respect for you, and that isn't acceptable."

Unfortunately, I've heard many variations on Lauren's story in my practice. She left our session a bit dazed, admitting she'd never thought about respect when it came to her personal relationships. "There can be no real love without respect," I told her.

Respect must be earned. We admire people because of their accomplishments or their character. Bosses earn our respect through their professional behavior and because they share their knowledge with us. Parents are respected when they raise us to be strong, loving, courteous, kind, and independent people. Governments are respected when they protect and defend the individual freedoms of their citizenry. Never allow yourself to be treated with a lack of respect. This will establish a destructive pattern, and you will become a resentful, angry person. You will find yourself living in a bubble of bad karma.

Take out a *yellow* index card and write:

Like attracts like. Self-respect is a magnet for respect.

Forgiveness

Forgiveness requires a great deal of strength. When we forgive, our hearts are filled with good karma. Forgiveness is refusing to bear a grudge; it releases hatred or resentment and lets go of any revengeful impulses. It is an act of love and illuminates our minds. It takes a great deal of energy to hate or to bear bad karmic wishes upon someone. Holding a grudge causes distress, colors our happiness, and creates bad karma. Bearing a grudge or performing a vengeful act will boomerang big time, bringing about an enormous deficit in our karmic bank account. Each time we forgive even the slightest injustice, we add good karma that goes toward clearing our debts, bringing our account closer to balance.

Lawrence told me about a good tool to use if we need to train our minds to be forgiving. "Each night before you go to bed, you must forgive everyone who has done you an injustice. You have heard that it is unwise to go to bed angry at your husband or wife. This should apply to everyone. You should think about the injustice and tell yourself that you hold no malice in your heart. You pardon everyone. This will make peace with those who have hurt you, and it will also give you inner peace."

Take out two *yellow* index cards and write:

1. Forgiveness is living in a state of grace.
2. The only time we are totally happy is when we have forgiven everyone.

Service

Any act of service is a deposit into the universal karmic bank. The only time we are totally happy is when we forget ourselves through serving others. Whenever we are busy serving the needs of someone else, we are creating good karma. Service will influence our own karma, as well as that of the people we serve. By such action we allow them greater peace of mind in order to promote balance in their lives.

When we pick up garbage on the street, we are serving the environment. When we vote, we are serving our country. When we listen to someone who needs to speak, we serve that person. Any action performed that benefits others contributes to the collective good karma of the universe. Each of us has the ability to perform a service that will move the world a little closer to karmic balance.

KARMA IN BALANCE

Practically speaking, karma is the name given to the operation of universal balance. What goes around comes around; you do indeed reap what you sow. Each moment of life gives us the opportunity to become more balanced, to create new, good karma—to take another step on the path toward self-mastery. This process moves us from our past lives, through this life, and into our next lives. Despite the fact that we cannot change the past, the future is ours to shape. We should be comforted knowing there's always another chance. There is no hurry. We have eternity in front of us. No one can do better than his or her best.

We can begin at this moment to live a happier, richer life, one that adds a vast amount to our karmic bank account. We can work toward greater balance in all areas of our lives—health, sex, money, and power. We will return to learn a few more lessons, search for a bit more truth, do as much as we can for others, and move a little closer toward perfection. We will finish this life, leave for a while, return, pick up our bankbook, and continue our journey in pursuit of balance. And as incredible as it may seem, in time all karmic debts will be paid, all earthly lives will be lived, total enlightenment achieved, and self-mastery attained.

LIST OF AFFIRMATIONS

CHAPTER 1 KARMA

Uncontrolled anger creates negative karma. It is destructive to my health, my work, my friends, my family, and my soul. I will find ways to control my rage.

CHAPTER 2 KARMA AND REINCARNATION

Karma means action. Good action brings forth good karma.

Karma means action. Bad action brings forth bad karma.

I see more bad karma than good when my behavior is more selfish than selfless.

I am my karma.

I am what I am because of my past thoughts, actions, and desires.

I am building my future by my present thoughts, actions, and desires.

Noble actions and constructive thinking create positive karma.

I will not waste time getting angry because I can't remember my past lives.

We learn the most about past lives by looking at this one.

Abilities can be a greater confirmation of past lives than memories.

A problem that I have right now does not have to remain one my whole life.

A true déjà vu is linked to something from a past life that I must resolve.

Be patient. It takes time to unlock memories that are hidden in our subconscious minds.

Always reflect on your present-life patterns before delving into the realms of past-life possibilities.

If a person receives accurate past life information, the effect will be seen in the present one.

Where there is life, there is hope.

You don't die, so you can't kill yourself.

Karma has no deadline.

CHAPTER 3   KARMA AND HEALTH

I will respect my body and my mind so that I can live with the harmony of greater health.

I will do my very best never to infect another person with any illness.

The karma for deception is a heavy one.

Excessive, compulsive exercise is a misuse of vital force.

You are given only a certain amount of vital force in a lifetime. Don't waste it!

Focus on the solution instead of the problem.

Hatred is always detrimental to health.

Any physical problem is the working out of karma rooted in this life or a past life.

I will deal with this test minute by minute.

If I don't overcome my addiction in this life, I will be born with it in the next one.

The power of the will lies in my individual skill in directing it.

Every day I will focus on my goal and fight for it.

My ultimate goal is to live so that I can relish this life and the next ones as a better person.

I will change my point of view from one of deprivation to one of integration.

CHAPTER 4   KARMA AND SEX

Passion without a firm foundation delivers a heavy punch to our judgment.

I will act with the highest principles of unselfishness. Only this can save my marriage from the state it has fallen into.

Karma has no victims.

I vow that under no circumstances will I become intimate with anyone I meet for an absolute minimum of forty days.

The past can't be changed, but I can alter the way I let it affect me in the present.

Kundalini energy follows the direction of thought.

Think beauty, harmony, balance, and service, and the road will be crystal clear.

Computers don't cheat. People cheat.

Typing is not dating.

Nobody dies, and nothing can be deleted.

You can't live without food and water, but you can live without sex.

CHAPTER 5   KARMA AND MONEY

Gratitude is the first rule of spiritual development.

True self-esteem can be obtained only through living in balance.

Obsession can lead to insanity.

An obsessive thought must be replaced with a constructive one.

A constructive thought is one that promotes health and peace of mind.

Never ignore any opportunity to help someone.

The next person who needs assistance could be you.

I can't erase bad karma, but I can learn and begin this moment to create good karma.

Positive thinking combined with appropriate action brings good karma.

I will do everything humanly possible to pay all my debts before I even consider bankruptcy.

If I abuse money in this life, I will be born with none in the next one.

There can be no erasures in the universal karma bank.

Debts have no deadline.

The homeless person you neglect could be you in another life.

CHAPTER 6   KARMA AND POWER

Power should have a positive position in my life.

Genuine power is reflected in my internal qualities.

I will not be a slave to ambition.

I will focus my energy on excellence, not on pursuing power.

History is a record of the human struggle.

Today's action is tomorrow's history.

Self-knowledge is the beginning of power.

I ask my higher self to help me to gain the power to overcome any barriers that keep me from personal happiness.

Real power is rooted in detachment.

Real power is based on integrity.

There is power in patience.

Do anything in your power to avert harm. This creates good karma.

A selfless person who owns power controls himself.

If you hear a cry for help, it's your karma to answer it.

The power to see another person's point of view is real power.

CHAPTER 7   KARMA AND BALANCE

All work performed in the spirit of harmony promotes balance.

I can and will find work that I delight in.

A life in which every day you have to debit your karma account is tragic because it is wasteful.

Waste produces bad karma.

A tree will grow as it is rooted.

All that you have earned will come to you.

I won't blame karma for my laziness and lack of dedication.

The universe is not responsible for my unfulfilled dreams. I am.

Unkindness always creates bad karma, because it's based in selfishness.

Without patience life is one long lament.

Talents and relationships must be free to bloom in their own time.

I will not be in such a hurry that I miss the beauty of the moment.

Like attracts like. Self-respect is a magnet for respect.

Forgiveness is living in a state of grace.

The only time we are totally happy is when we have forgiven everyone.